Best Bike Rides Around Portland

by Anndy Wiselogle and Virginia Church

First printing May 1987
Second printing August 1987
Third printing February 1989
Fourth printing April 1990

Cover design by Martha Gannett
Photographs by Jerome Hart

Published by the Bicycle Commuter Service
4438 S.E. Belmont Street
Portland, Oregon 97215

ISBN 0-9618290-0-1

Table of Contents

Map Symbols

 Trip route

 Bike path

 Gravel road

 Other roads

 Grocery store

 Restaurant

 Campground

Introduction

Well, if Portland isn't one of the best starting points for a bike ride! Right around the corner there are peaceful lakes, challenging hills, ferry boats, old pioneer cabins, mountain views, unique bakeries, bird refuges, rainbows, waterfalls, . . .

But wait—one of the finest joys of a good bike ride is discovering these things yourself. A bike ride is an experience, an interaction between you, your bicycle and your route. Our purpose is to suggest a good bike route, and let you see what's there yourself.

We've collected 34 of the area's best bike rides, including some old favorites and some new discoveries of our own. All are written as loops that return to the starting point. Most rides start in Portland, and a dozen rides start in neighboring towns.

The rides are organized into four groups: Easy Rides, Moderate Rides, Challenging Rides, and Most Difficult Rides. The category for each ride was based on the hills, the length, and how we felt after doing the loop. Rides suitable for overnight camping trips are included at the back of each section.

We have tried to make the maps and mileage logs as clear and accurate as possible. However we have learned a great truth that applies to these routes: things will change. Odometers vary, street names change, new roads are built, and traffic patterns will change. Use this book as a good guide, but if the road seems different than we indicate, it may well be different. If a route becomes undesirable, by all means don't follow it.

These routes take you along bike paths, rural roads, scenic highways, and some busy streets. In all cases we insist that bicyclists ride safely and follow the rules of the road. Always ride on the right, stop at stop signs and red lights, use arm signals to indicate turns, be aware of traffic around you and share the roadways. Those who wear bicycle helmets have added protection and are more visible.

With this book we have tried to share our joy of cycling around the Portland area. The discoveries are there waiting to be found. So choose a ride, hop on your bike, and see what's around that next corner.

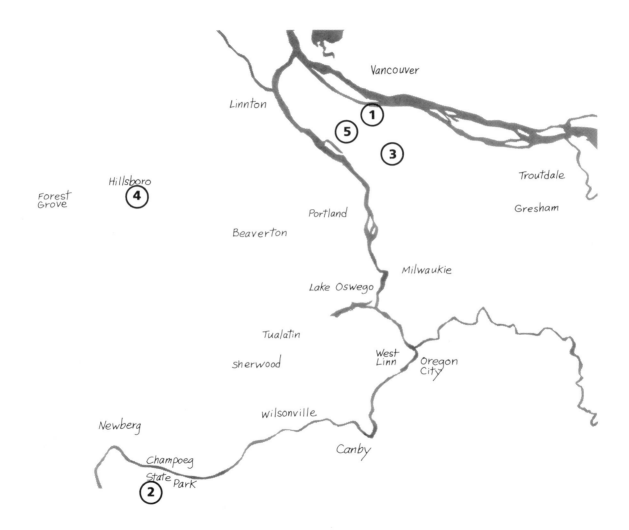

Vancouver

Linnton

① 5 ③

Troutdale

Hillsboro ④

Forest Grove

Gresham

Portland

Beaverton

Milwaukie

Lake Oswego

Tualatin

Sherwood

West Linn

Oregon City

Wilsonville

Newberg

Champoeg State Park ②

Canby

Easy Rides

1 Columbia River

21 miles
from north Portland
easy

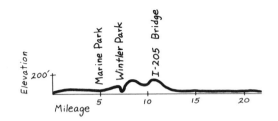

From a small lake in the Canadian Rockies, the Columbia River begins its 1200-mile descent through deep gorges, rapids, and several hydroelectric dams. Near Portland, where the river continues its last 100 miles, it's only a few feet above sea level, and the roadways along either side are fairly level. The terrain and the views make this exceptional for a nice easy ride (although there are a couple short steep hills).

This ride shows off both sides of the Columbia, with two waterfront parks, wonderful views of the river and its inhabitants, and many miles of official bicycle routes. There is, however, a short section along busy Highway 14 in Washington, where you should ride on the shoulder.

0.0 Start in **East Delta Park** in north Portland, by the restrooms near the playing fields. Ride north and east as the road curves under Highway 99E. Follow the bike route signs toward Vancouver.

0.3 Turn **left** at **Vancouver Way**, then **left** on **Marine Drive**.

0.4 Turn **right** to stay on the **bike route**.

0.6 The **bike route** crosses **left** across Marine Drive and up onto the bridge over the slough. Keep following the signs for the bike route as it meanders around to get you to the bridge.

1.4 Start on the sidewalk bike route on the I-5 bridge.

2.3 Bike path ends at T-intersection at **Columbia Street**, turn **left**, under the I-5 bridge.

2.7 Turn **right** into Broughton Park just after the restaurant to ride the short length of bike path along the river's edge. Then continue east on Columbia Way.

3.7 You come upon Columbia Industrial Park, where there's a bike path on the right side of the street for a mile and a half. There are also several railroad tracks to cross; watch those skinny tires!

4.8 Road curves right to become **Marine Park Way**.

5.3 **Marine Park**—restrooms, beach, boat ramp, picnicking. Turn around and ride along Marine Park Way.

5.8 Turn **right** to continue on Marine Park Way, toward the railroad undercrossing.

5.9 Stop sign at **Highway 14**, turn **right**. This is busy so stay on the shoulder.

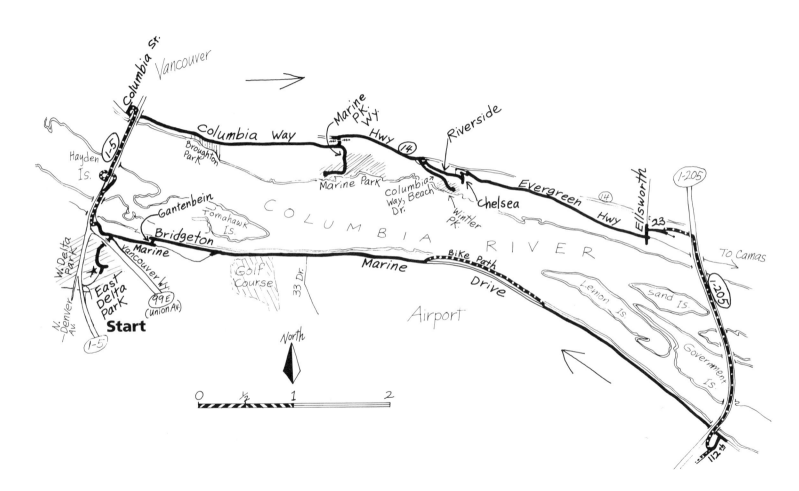

Columbia St.

Vancouver

Columbia Way

Marine PK. WY.

Hwy 14

Riverside

I-5

Hayden Is.

Broughton Park

Marine Park

Columbia Way, Beach Dr.

Winter PK.

Chelsea

Evergreen Hwy

14

Ellsworth

23

I-205

Gantenbein

Tomahawk Is.

Bridgeton

Marine

Vancouver Wy.

99 E (Union Av.)

W. Delta Park

East Delta Park

N. Denver Av.

I-5

Start

C O L U M B I A   R I V E R

Golf Course

33 Dr.

Marine

Drive

Bike Path

Airport

Lemon Is.

sand Is.

Government Is.

To Camas

I-205

112

North

0   ½   1   2

6.8 Take the **first exit** (Exit 3), to Wintler County Park. Turn **right** from the exit, and immediately turn **left** to the Dead End with the sign pointing to Beach Drive (this street is Columbia Way).

7.3 **Wintler Park**—river access, restrooms, picnicking (open in summer). Turn around after relaxing in the park and head back up the hill.

7.7 Turn **right**, and **right** again to **Riverside Drive**.

8.1 Turn **left** on **Chelsea Avenue**, as the bike route sign points.

8.2 T-intersection at **Evergreen Highway**, turn **right**.

10.3 Turn **left** on **Ellsworth Avenue**.

10.4 Turn **right** on **23rd Street**.

10.6 Turn **left** onto the **bike route**, and over the Columbia River.

13.4 T-intersection in the bike path, turn **left** to Marine Drive.

13.6 Bike route ends at **Marine Drive**, turn **left**.

15.1 Turn **right** onto the **bike route**, part of the 40-Mile Loop.

17.7 Bike route ends, continue on Marine Drive.

19.6 Where Marine Drive curves left, take the **right fork—Bridgeton Road**.

20.3 Turn **left** on **Gantenbein Avenue**, just before Bridgeton ends.

20.4 T-intersection at **Marine Drive**, turn **right**.

20.8 Turn **left** at **Marine Way**, toward Delta Park.

21.1 **Delta Park** restrooms, end of loop.

2 French Prairie

28 miles
from Champoeg Park, south of Wilsonville
easy

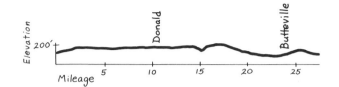

While the French Prairie area south of Champoeg Park is not quite Portland's back yard, it's certainly a close neighbor and well worth its friendship, especially for a bicyclist. The roads are quiet and flat, the scenery is varied and intriguing, and this loop takes you along the bike path through Champoeg Park.

0.0 **Champoeg Park** is the starting point. (You can ride your bike there via the Champoeg Park ride, or drive there on I-5, taking Exit 278 and following the signs to the park.) Start from the Visitor Center and Museum, situated to the right after the entrance to the park. Turn **right** as you leave the park.

0.3 Turn **left** on **French Prairie Road**.

4.0 Stop sign at **St. Paul Highway**, turn **left** toward Hubbard.

8.1 T-intersection at **Butteville Road**, turn **left** toward Donald.

10.4 Town of Donald. Turn **right** at the stop sign onto **Donald Road**.

14.5 Stop sign at **Ehlen Road**, turn **right**, then go across the highway.

15.4 Turn **left** on **Airport Road**, toward Wilsonville.

17.4 Cross Arndt Road.

19.1 T-intersection at **Miley Road**, turn **left**. This becomes Butteville Road.

22.3 Willamette Greenway Park is on the right.

24.5 Town of Butteville. Stop sign at **Butteville Road** (don't be confused by all the Butteville Roads in the same area; these directions do work), turn **right** toward Champoeg Park.

24.7 Turn **right** on **Schuler Road**.

25.1 Turn **left** onto the **bike path** through Champoeg Park.

27.0 Turn **right** on the road, and follow the bike path to the Visitor Center.

27.5 Turn **left** across the road on the bike path and cross the creek.

27.7 Return to the Visitor Center area.

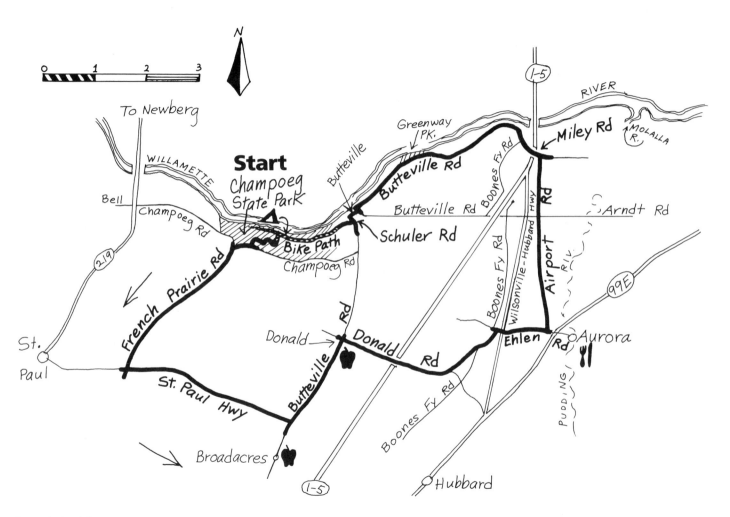

Hops

In the summer the 20-foot vines of hops draw your attention and your questions. The hop is a perennial plant, sending vines up in a clockwise direction around its support, growing up to one foot a day. The cones of female flowers are harvested in late August or early September, dried, and then used in the process of making beer. Hops give beer its distinctive flavor and aroma.

3 Kelley Point Park

34 miles
from northeast Portland
easy

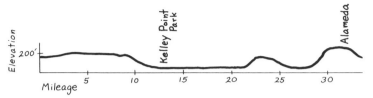

There aren't many cities that can boast a bike ride like this one through Portland. First of all, Kelley Point Park is a vast area along the confluence of the Willamette and Columbia Rivers where you can watch the foreign ocean ships going by. Second, you pass through urban wildlife areas where you should see herons, kingfishers, muskrats and rabbits. And third, this ride is along some of the most pleasant, level, uninterrupted streets in the city.

All this and good exercise too!

0.0 Start at **Grant Park**, N.E. 33rd and U.S. Grant Place, in Portland. Ride west on U.S. Grant Place.
0.2 T-intersection at **28th Avenue**, turn **right**.
0.5 T-intersection at **Knott Street**, turn **left**.
1.7 T-intersection at **Union Avenue**, turn **left**, then immediately **right** to stay on **Knott Street**.
2.0 Stop sign at **Williams Avenue**, turn **right**.
3.5 Williams Avenue turns left to **Jessup Street**.
3.6 Turn **right** on **Vancouver Avenue**.
3.8 Traffic signal at **Ainsworth Street**, turn **left**.
5.3 T-intersection at **Willamette Boulevard**, turn **right**.
8.6 Stop sign at Richmond Avenue, go **straight** on **Willamette Boulevard**.
9.6 Turn **right** on **Reno Avenue**.
9.7 Stop sign on **Lombard Street**, turn **left**. This is called Burgard Road after the railroad tracks.
11.0 Turn **left** at the sign "To Rivergate Industrial District" as the road curves right. This is later called Lombard Street.
13.4 Turn **left** into **Kelley Point Park** after crossing the slough bridge.
14.1 Main parking lot of Kelley Point Park. Walk through to see the river, to picnic, to swim, to hike. After your visit, return back via the road that brought you in.
14.8 T-intersection at the park entrance (Marine Drive), turn **left**.
18.2 T-intersection on **Portland Road**, turn **left**. This is called Marine Drive after the railroad tracks.
19.4 Turn **right** on **N. Force Avenue**, marked by the sign "West Delta Park."
20.0 Turn **left** on the unmarked road before the gate (Broadacre Street).

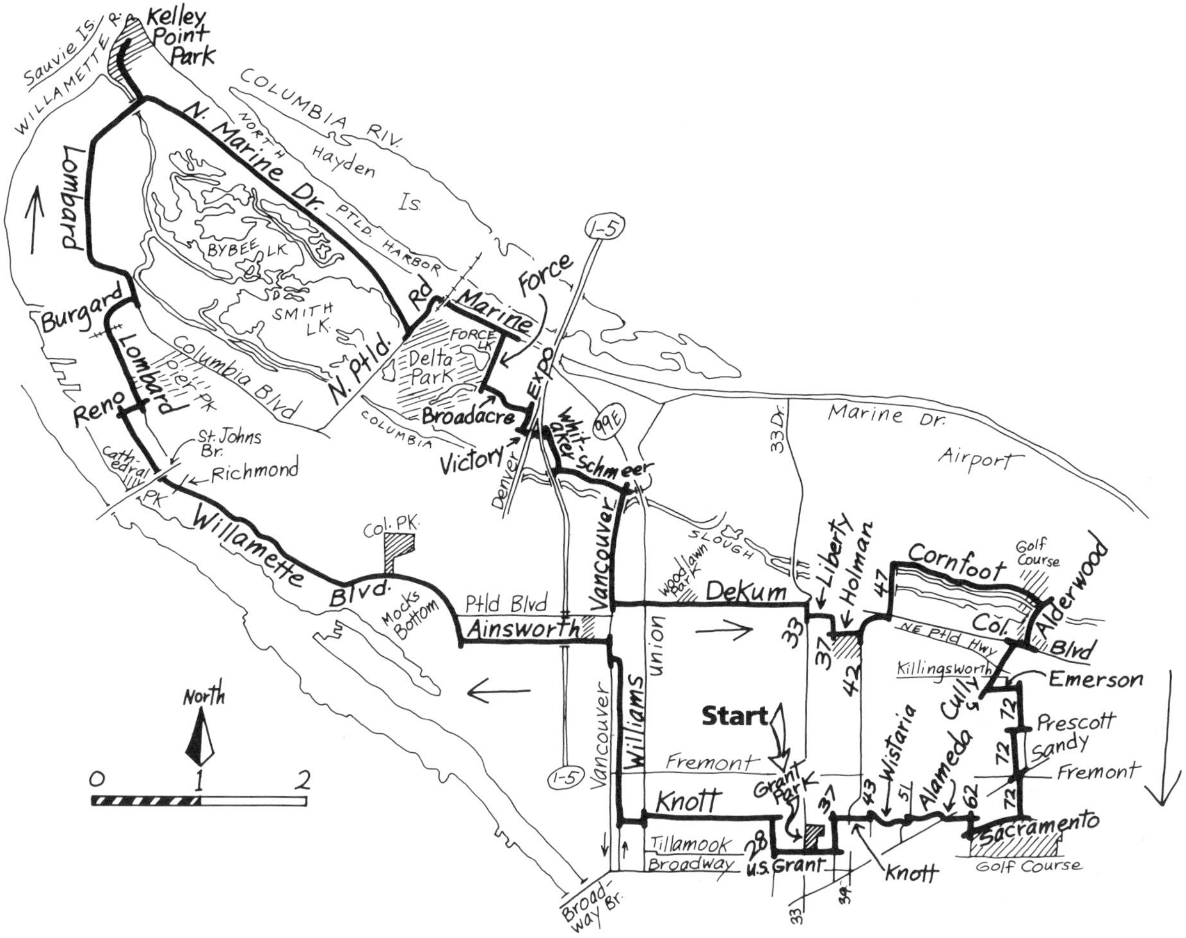
Kelley Point Park
Sauvie Is.
Willamette R.
Columbia Riv.
North Hayden Is.
Ptld. Harbor
N. Marine Dr.
Lombard
Bybee Lk
Smith Lk.
Burgard
Columbia Blvd
Pier Pk
Reno
N. Ptld. Rd
Marine
Force
Force Lk
Delta Park
Broadacre
Expo
I-5
Victory
Denver
Whitaker
99E
Schmeer
St. Johns Br.
Richmond
Cathedral Pk
Willamette Blvd.
Col. Pk.
Mocks Bottom
Ptld Blvd
Ainsworth
Vancouver
Williams
Union
Woodlawn Park
Slough
DeKum
33
Liberty
Holman
37
42
47
Cornfoot
Golf Course
Alderwood
Col. Blvd
NE Ptld Hwy
Killingsworth
Emerson
Cully
72
Prescott
Sandy
Fremont
Marine Dr.
33 Dr.
Airport
Start
Grant Park
Wistaria
Alameda
43
51
62
Knott
Sacramento
Tillamook
Broadway
28
U.S. Grant
Broadway Br.
North
0 1 2

20.6 T-intersection at unmarked road (Expo Road), turn **right**.

20.8 T-intersection at **Victory Boulevard**, turn **left** and go under the freeway.

21.0 The road curves right onto **Whitaker Road**.

21.5 T-intersection on **Schmeer Road**, turn **left**.

22.2 Stop sign at **Vancouver Avenue**, turn **right**.

23.2 Turn **left** on **Dekum Street**, before the school.

25.1 Stop sign at **33rd Avenue**, turn **right**.

25.2 Turn **left** on **Liberty Street**.

25.6 Liberty Street curves right and becomes **37th Avenue**.

25.7 Stop sign on **Holman Street**, turn **left**.

25.9 Stop sign on **42nd Avenue**, turn **left** and follow the sign "To Columbia Boulevard" (42nd curves into 47th Avenue).

26.3 Cross Columbia Boulevard at the signal.

26.8 Turn **right** on **Cornfoot Road**.

28.3 T-intersection at **Alderwood Road**, turn **right**.

28.7 Flashing red light at **Columbia Boulevard**, turn **right**.

28.8 Turn **left** on **Cully Boulevard**.

29.3 Turn **left** on **Emerson Street**.

29.6 T-intersection at **72nd Avenue**, turn **right**.

30.0 Stop sign at Prescott Street, **jog right** to stay on **72nd Avenue**.

30.5 Traffic signal at Sandy Boulevard, **jog left** to keep on **72nd Avenue**.

30.9 T-intersection at **Sacramento Street**, turn **right**.

31.4 Turn **right** on **62nd Avenue**.

31.7 Turn **left** on **Alameda**.

31.9 Cross Sandy Boulevard at the traffic signal, and stay on **Alameda**.

32.2 Turn **left** on **Wistaria Drive** (at 51st Avenue). Wistaria is the upper street running parallel to Alameda.

32.7 Turn **left** on **43rd Avenue**.

32.7 Turn **right** on **Knott Street**.

33.1 Stop sign at **37th Avenue**, turn **left**.

33.3 Turn **right** at **Tillamook/U.S. Grant Place**.

33.6 Return to **Grant Park**, 33rd and Grant Place.

4 Old Scotch Church

23 miles
from Shute Park in Hillsboro
easy

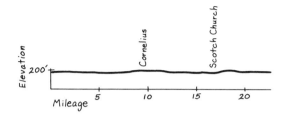

This ride takes you by several history-filled churches, of which the Old Scotch Church is the most striking in its setting. The rich Tualatin Valley farmland had several communities, and as you read their vestigial road signs you can imagine life here at the turn of the century.

This loop is relatively flat with little traffic and it makes an ideal pleasure ride. Be sure to partake of the fresh fruits at one of the several produce stands en route.

0.0 Start at **Shute Park** in Hillsboro on 10th Avenue and Maple Street. Head east on Maple Street, crossing with the traffic signal.
0.6 Turn **right** on **21st Avenue**. This becomes Minter Bridge Road.
3.7 Stop sign at **Grabel Road**, turn **right**.
4.0 T-intersection at **Highway 219**, turn **right** toward the golf course.
4.3 Turn **left** on **Tongue Lane**.
7.4 Turn **right** on **Golf Course Road**. This becomes 10th Avenue in Cornelius, then Cornelius-Schefflin Road.
12.7 Turn **right** on **Cornelius-Schefflin Road** (Verboort Road goes straight). This becomes Zion Church Road, then Scotch Church Road.
17.0 The Old Scotch Church is on the left.
18.3 T-intersection at **Jackson Road**, turn **right**.
19.9 T-intersection at **Evergreen Street**, turn **right**.
20.2 Turn **left** on **Jackson Road**. This becomes Jackson School Road.
21.8 Turn **left** on **5th Avenue**.
22.6 Turn **left** on **Walnut Street**.
22.8 Turn **right** on **7th Avenue**.
22.9 Turn **left** on **Maple Street**.
23.2 Return to **Shute Park**.

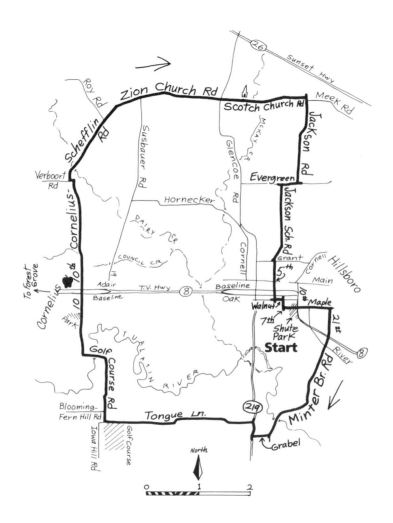

5 Sauvie Island

28 miles
from north Portland
easy

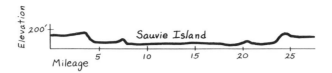

There's something alluring about riding your bike on an island. And there's something especially attractive about Sauvie Island. Maybe it's the peaceful views over the fields and the river, or maybe it's the large area dedicated to a wildlife preserve, or maybe just the flat roads that amble around the island. For lots of reasons the Sauvie Island loop is one that is on the recommended riding list.

Besides the loop, the three paved roads on the island are excellent out-and-back trips. Sauvie Island Road leads you along the Multnomah Channel out to Steelman Lake. Oak Island Road leads to a good bird-watching area. And Reeder Road goes out to the sandy beaches.

0.0 Start at **Columbia Park**, N. Lombard and Woolsey Avenue in Portland. Go south on Woolsey.
0.2 T-intersection at **Willamette Boulevard**, turn **right**.
2.4 Stop sign at **Richmond Avenue**, turn **right**.
2.6 Stop sign at **Ivanhoe Street**, turn **left**.
2.8 Traffic signal at **Philadelphia Avenue**, turn **left** and cross the St. Johns Bridge. You may use the sidewalk over the bridge.
3.6 Traffic signal at the end of the bridge, turn **right**.
4.0 Traffic signal at **Highway 30** (St. Helens Road), turn **left**.
7.5 Traffic signal at the **Sauvie Island Bridge**, turn **right**.
7.8 Turn **left** on **Gillihan Road**, and loop under the bridge.
14.0 Stop sign at **Reeder Road**, turn **left**. Or follow Reeder Road north (turn right) along the Columbia River to the beach area.
17.1 Oak Island Road comes in on the right.
18.4 Stop sign at **Sauvie Island Road**, turn **left**. Or turn right to ride along the dike by the Multnomah Channel.
20.1 Go **straight** at the fork and ride over the bridge.
20.4 Traffic signal at **Highway 30**, turn **left**.
23.9 Turn **right** to the **St. Johns Bridge** (Bridge Avenue).
24.3 Traffic light at the **St. Johns Bridge**, turn **left**. You may use the sidewalk.
25.1 Traffic signal at **Ivanhoe Street**, turn **right**.
25.3 Turn **right** on **Richmond Avenue**.
25.5 Turn **left** on **Willamette Boulevard**.
27.7 Turn **left** on **Woolsey Avenue**.
27.9 Return to **Columbia Park** on Lombard Street.

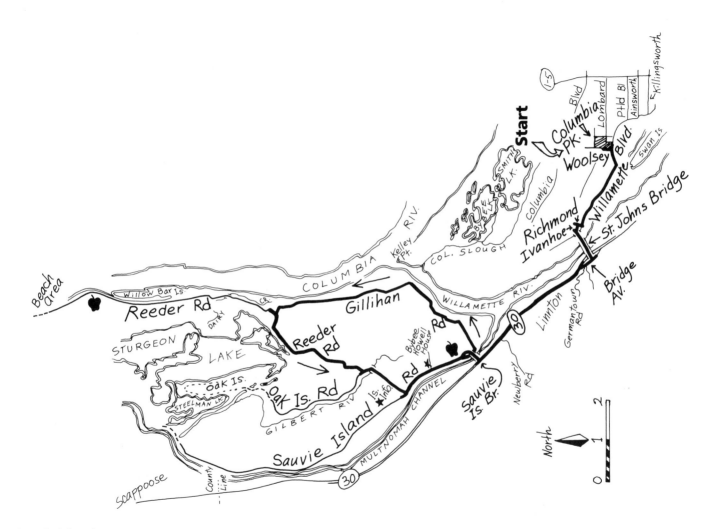

The sandhill crane, a glorious three-foot tall dusty-gray bird, migrates through Sauvie Island in the fall, eating field grain and small rodents. This bird lives up to 70 years, with a female-male pair coupled for life. Both parents incubate the eggs and care for the young. In the fall you can hear their distinctive "ga-roo" call while they fly in a V-formation overhead.

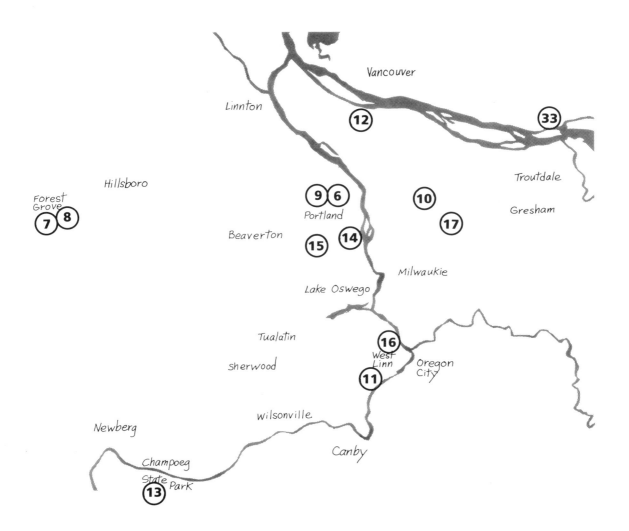

Moderate Rides

6 Council Crest

15 miles
from northwest Portland
moderate

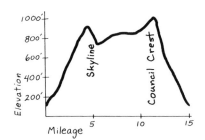

Here's a ride to show off Portland to your visiting relatives, assuming they can ride up hills. Washington Park is always a show piece, and what better view of it than from a bicycle? The Fairmount Boulevard loop is a favorite for riding, and it's crowned by Council Crest Park, overlooking mountains to the east and the valley to the west. The finale is a downhill coast, all the way back to the park. Your relatives will love it!

0.0 Begin at Portland's **Wallace Park**, N.W. 25th and Raleigh Street. Go south on 25th Avenue.
0.4 Stop sign at **Westover Road**, angle slightly **left**.
0.7 Stop sign at **23rd Place**, turn **right**.
0.7 Stop sign at **Burnside Street**, turn **right** (or cross Burnside here and use the sidewalk).
0.8 Turn **left** on **Sterns Road** (unmarked), the first left after the fountain.
1.2 T-intersection at **Washington Way**, turn **right**.
1.4 Take the **right fork** downhill.
1.5 Stop sign at Rose Garden Boulevard, unmarked, go **straight**, toward the zoo.
2.0 Stop sign at **Kingston Drive**, go **straight** following the sign to the zoo.
3.6 T-intersection at **Knights Boulevard**, turn **right**.
3.8 T-intersection at **Fairview Boulevard**, turn **left**.
4.4 T-intersection at **Skyline Boulevard**, turn **left**.
5.2 Traffic signals where you cross over the Sunset Highway. Use the center lane through the last set of signals to go straight on **Hewett Boulevard** (also signed 58th Avenue).
7.0 T-intersection at **Patton Road**, turn **left**.
7.1 Stop sign at **Talbot Road**, turn **right**.
7.2 Stop sign at **Fairmount Boulevard**, turn **right**.
9.6 Marquam Hill Road comes in, stay left.
10.6 Turn **left** under the overpass on **Talbot Road**.

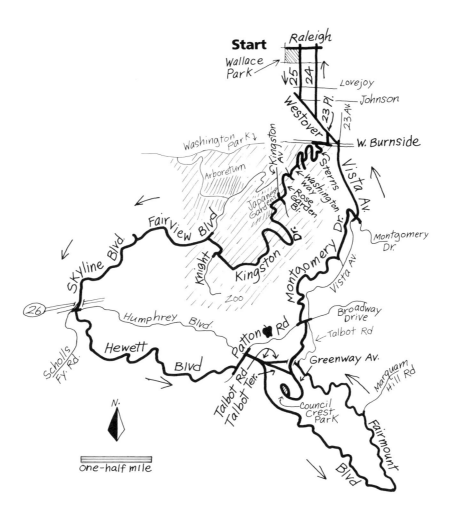

Start

Raleigh

Wallace Park

25 24

Lovejoy

Johnson

Westover

23 Pl.

23 Av.

W. Burnside

Washington Park

Kingston Av.

Sterns

Vista Av.

Arboretum

Washington Way

Rose Garden Bl.

Japanese Gardens

Montgomery Dr.

Fairview Blvd.

Kingston Dr.

Skyline Blvd.

Knight

Kingston

Montgomery Dr.

Vista Av.

26

Humphrey Blvd.

Zoo

Broadway Drive

Talbot Rd

Scholls Fy. Rd.

Hewett

Blvd

Patton Rd.

Greenway Av.

Marquam Hill Rd

N.

Talbot Rd.—Talbot Ter.

Council Crest Park

Fairmount Blvd

one-half mile

10.8 Turn **left** (U-turn) on **Talbot Terrace.**

10.9 T-intersection at **Greenway Avenue**, turn **right**.

11.2 Turn **right** on **Council Crest Drive**, marked "Dead End." Ride around the Council Crest loop and return.

11.8 Stop sign at **Greenway Avenue**, turn **left.**

12.4 Stop sign at **Patton Road**, turn **left** for one block.

12.5 Turn **right** on **Montgomery Drive** (follow the street signs to stay on Montgomery Drive, which curves around).

13.7 Stop sign at **Vista Avenue**, turn **left**.

14.4 Traffic signal at Burnside Street at the bottom of the hill, cross Burnside and angle slightly **left** on **Westover Road**.

14.5 Turn **right** at the fork on **24th Avenue**.

15.1 Turn **left** on **Raleigh Street**.

15.2 Return to **Wallace Park**, 25th and Raleigh.

7 Hagg Lake

**27 miles
from Forest Grove
moderate**

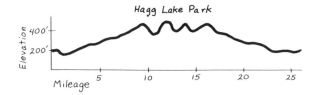

This large and beautiful lake with its surrounding mountains gives you a feeling of being in some exotic faraway place. The lake was created for water control and recreational purposes, and the park is dotted with creeks, trails, swimming beaches, and scenic picnic areas. The somewhat hilly road around the lake has wide shoulders marked for bicycles.

This is one of those spots that readily draws scores of bicyclists on the first warm sunny day in May, but take note that during the off-season winter months there is virtually no motorized traffic, and the only other ones on the road may be the orange-bellied salamanders.

0.0 Start at **Rogers Park**, on 17th Avenue and Elm Street in Forest Grove. Head west on 17th Avenue.
0.5 Stop sign at **B Street**, turn **left**.
1.4 Turn **right** onto Old Highway 47 (marked "To Hiatt Road").
1.9 Stop sign at **Highway 47**, turn **right**.
2.8 Turn **right** at the sign "Old TV Highway."
5.0 Stop sign at **Scoggins Valley Road**, turn **right** toward the park.
7.8 Continue straight to begin the loop around Hagg Lake.
18.2 T-intersection at Scoggins Valley Road, turn **right** toward Forest Grove.
20.8 Turn **left** at **Old Highway 47**.
23.0 T-intersection at **Highway 47**, turn **left**.
23.2 Turn **right** on **Anderson Road**.
24.2 Cross Highway 47.
24.7 T-intersection at **Highway 47**, turn **left**. This becomes B Street.
25.5 Turn **right** on **17th Street**.
26.1 Return to **Rogers Park** at Elm Street.

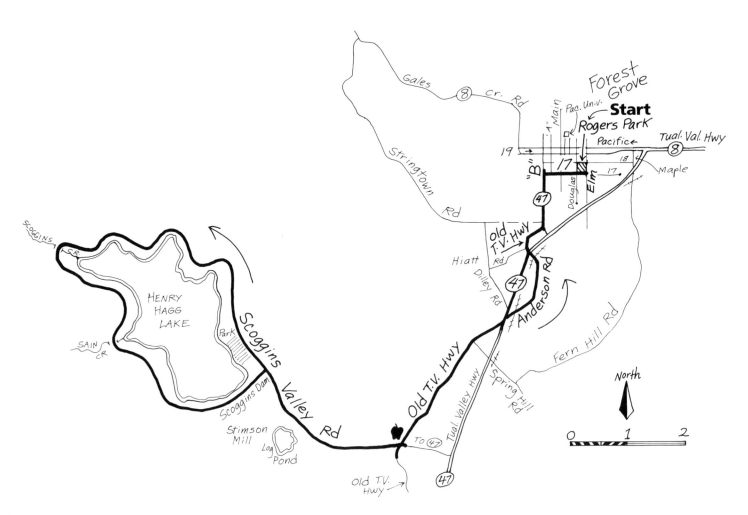

Gales Cr. Rd
8
Forest Grove
"A" Main
Pac. Univ.
Start
Rogers Park
Pacific
Tual. Val. Hwy
8
19
"B"
17
18
Elm
17
Maple
Douglas
47
Stringtown Rd
Old T.V. Hwy
47
Hiatt
Rd
Diley Rd
47
Anderson Rd
Fern Hill Rd
SCOGGINS
H.S.R.
HENRY HAGG LAKE
Park
SAIN CR.
Scoggins Valley Rd
Scoggins Dam
Stimson Mill
Log Pond
Old T.V. Hwy
Tual. Valley Hwy
Spring Hill Rd
To 47
Old T.V. Hwy
47

North

0   1   2

8 Hillsides/Farmlands

25 miles
from Forest Grove
moderate

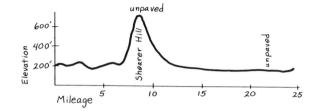

As you get farther from the populated metropolitan areas you get a better feel for the fertile, colorful, and quiet land of the Northwest. This loop shows off Oregon's walnut and filbert crops, strawberry fields, apple orchards, dairy farms, and even gives a glimpse at the forest lands. You get the overall perspective from atop Shearer Hill, and then you ride right through the patchwork fields you observed.

About four miles of roads are not paved (including a short stretch on a closed road), and it's on adventures like this that you find the best scenes and the least traffic.

0.0 Begin at **College Avenue** and **University Way** by Pacific University in Forest Grove. Head west on University Way.
0.0 T-intersection at **Main Street**, turn **right**.
0.1 Turn **left** on **23rd Avenue**.
0.6 Stop sign at **E Street**, turn **right**. This becomes Gales Creek Road.
1.1 Turn **right** at the fork onto **Thatcher Road**.
3.9 Turn **left** on **Hillside Road**.
7.4 T-intersection at **Clapshaw Hill Road**, turn **left**.
7.9 Turn **right** on **Shearer Road**.
8.4 Unpaved road begins.
9.0 Turn **right** on **Strohmayer Road**, and continue through the Closed Road sign.
9.8 Continue straight on Strohmayer Road.
10.5 Road is paved.
12.9 Turn **left** on **Greenville-Roy Road**.
16.4 T-intersection at **Roy Road**, turn **right**.
19.1 T-intersection at **Cornelius-Schefflin Road**, turn **right**.
20.4 T-intersection at **Verboort Road**, turn **right**.
21.5 Turn **left** on **Porter Road** (unpaved).
23.5 Turn **right** on **22nd Avenue**.
24.0 T-intersection at **Hawthorne Street**, turn **left**.
24.2 Turn **right** on **21st Avenue**.
24.5 T-intersection at **Cedar Street**, turn **right**.
24.7 Turn **left** on **23rd Avenue**, which becomes University Way.
24.9 Return to the start at **College Avenue** and **University Way**.

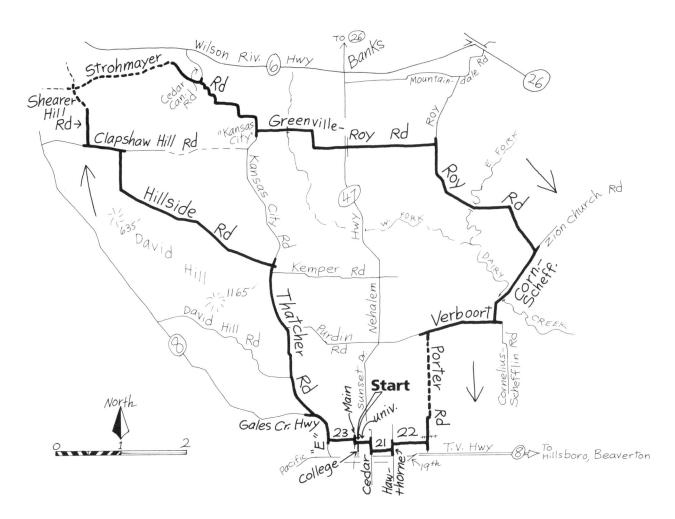

9 Leif Erikson Drive

19 miles
from northwest Portland
moderate

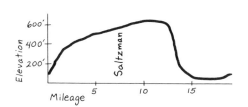

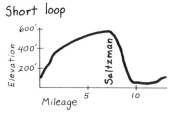

Short loop

The joy of Leif Erikson Drive (or the agony) is that it's an unpaved road through Portland's Forest Park. For eleven miles you get to (or, have to) pedal leisurely along the contour line in and out of the Tualatin Mountain ravines, with no other traffic in sight. Light-wheeled racing bikes may not enjoy it, but touring bikes and three-speeds have a good time, and mountain bikes are in heaven.

Forest Park is a unique asset for Portlanders. Its size (8 miles long and 1½ miles wide) makes it one of the largest urban parks in the country. Depending on the season, you can see trillium, bracken fern, dogwood, chickadees, woodpeckers, deer mice, and lots of chipmunks.

0.0 Start at Portland's **Wallace Park**, N.W. 25th and Raleigh Street. Go west on Raleigh Street.
0.1 Turn **right** on **27th Avenue**.
0.2 Stop sign at **Thurman Street**, turn **left**.
1.3 At the gate, Thurman Street becomes **Leif Erikson Drive**, which is unpaved.
7.5 Intersection with Saltzman Road. The next part of Leif Erikson is rougher. (If you want to head back, turn right on Saltzman, which is paved. Ride 2.0 miles to St. Helens Road where you turn right and continue the log from mile 15.8.) To continue on Leif Erikson, jog left through a gate, then right through another gate.
10.7 Intersection with Springville Road, continue straight.
12.6 T-intersection at **Germantown Road**, turn **right**.
13.8 Stop sign at **Bridge Avenue**, turn **right**.
14.7 Bridge Avenue merges into **St. Helens Road** (Highway 30).
15.8 Saltzman Road intersects St. Helens Road.
16.8 Traffic signal at Kittridge Avenue, turn **right** to stay on **St. Helens Road** (Highway 30).
18.4 Traffic signal at **29th Avenue**, turn **right**.
18.6 29th curves left into **Upshur Street**.
18.7 Turn **right** on **28th Avenue**.
18.7 Stop sign at **Thurman Street**, turn **left**.
18.9 Turn **right** on **27th Avenue**.
19.0 Turn **left** on **Raleigh Street**.
19.2 Back to **Wallace Park**, 25th and Raleigh Street.

North

one mile

Germantown Rd
Firelane 9
gate
Springville Rd
Leif Erikson
St. Johns Br.
Quarry Rd
St. Helens Rd
WILLAMETTE
U. of Portland
Swan Is.
RIV.
Saltzman
Leif
Erikson Dr.
Skyline Blvd
Thompson Rd
53 Dr.
Front Av.
Yeon
30
gate
Thurman
Corneil Rd
29 Upshur
28
Thurman
Raleigh
27
25
Lovejoy
Start
Wallace Park

10 Three Eastside Parks

35 miles
from southeast Portland
moderate

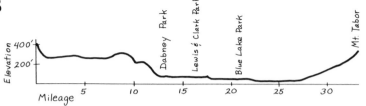

Not only are there spacious beautiful parks right in the city of Portland, but within a short jaunt you can get to several other wonderful and quite different parks. This tour from Mt. Tabor Park with its volcanic cinder cone takes you to see Dabney Park with its excitement of the Sandy River, Lewis and Clark Park with its awesome Broughton Bluff, and Blue Lake Park with its popular lake and picnic grounds.

Most of this route is along bike routes or on quiet streets, so getting there is half the fun!

0.0 Start at **Mt. Tabor Park**, S.E. 69th Avenue just south of Yamhill Street in Portland. Ride one block north to **Yamhill Street** and turn **right**.
0.4 Four-way stop sign at **76th Avenue**, turn **right**.
0.8 Turn **left** on **Stephens Street**.
1.0 T-intersection at **80th Avenue**, turn **left** and go one block.
1.1 Turn **right** on **Mill Street**.
1.7 Stop sign at **92nd Avenue**, turn **left**.
1.8 Turn **right** on **Market Street**.
3.7 T-intersection at **130th Avenue**, turn **right**.
3.8 Turn **left** on **Mill Street**, following the bike route. This becomes **Millmain Drive**, then **Main Street**.
6.4 Turn **left** on **179th Avenue**.
6.5 Stop sign at **Yamhill Street**, turn **right**. This curves into 197th Avenue.
7.5 Traffic light at **Burnside Street**, turn **right**. Shortly after you cross the light rail tracks, a bike lane begins.
8.8 Traffic light at **Eastman Parkway**, turn **left**.
8.9 Turn **right** on **Fairview Drive**, and then **left** on **20th Street**.
9.1 T-intersection at **Main Avenue**, jog **right** then **left** on **19th Street**.
9.6 Stop sign at Cleveland Avenue, **jog left** to get on **18th Street**.
9.9 T-intersection at **Hogan Drive**, turn **left**.
10.1 Turn **right** on **23rd Street**.
10.8 Stop sign at **Kane Drive**, turn **right**.

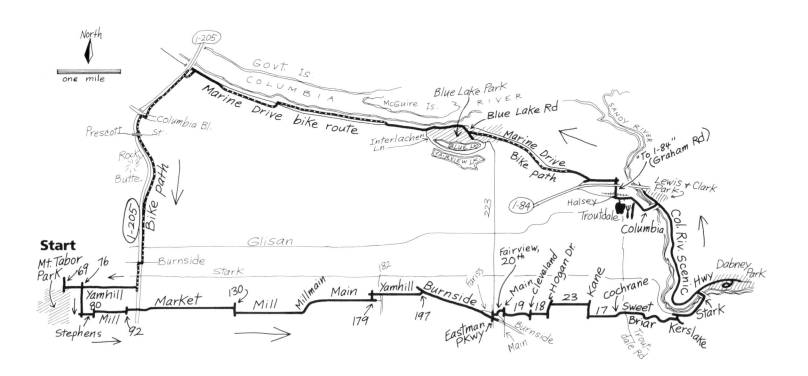

North

one mile

I-205

GOVT. IS.

COLUMBIA

Marine Drive bike route

McGuire Is.

Blue Lake Park

RIVER

Blue Lake Rd

Columbia Bl. St.

Prescott

Rocky Butte

I-205

Bike path

Interlachen Ln.

BLUE Lk.

FAIRVIEW Lk.

Marine Drive
Bike Path

"To I-84"
(Graham Rd)

SANDY RIVER

223

I-84

Halsey

Troutdale

Columbia

Lewis & Clark
Park

Col. Riv. Scenic

Glisan

Start

Mt. Tabor
Park

16

69

Burnside

Stark

182

Fairview,
20th

Dabney
Park

Yamhill
80

Market

130

Mill

Millmain

Main

179

197

Yamhill

Burnside

Eastman
PKWY

Fariss

Main

19

18

Cleveland

Hogan Dr.

23

Kane

Cochrane

17

Sweet
Briar

Kerslake

Trout-
dale Rd

Stark

Hwy

Mill
92

Stephens

Burnside

Main

11.1 Turn **left** on **17th Street**. This becomes **Cochrane**, then **Sweet Briar Road**.

12.5 Curve **left** to stay on **Sweet Briar Road**.

12.9 Turn **left** on **Kerslake Road**, in the middle of a good downhill run.

13.0 Stop sign at **Stark Street**, turn **right**.

13.6 T-intersection at the **Scenic Highway** just after crossing the bridge, turn **right**.

14.0 Turn **right** into **Dabney Park**, which offers picnicking, restrooms, and a good look at the Sandy River. After your break, retrace your route out the park, turning **left** on the **Scenic Highway**, and ride past the bridge you crossed earlier.

17.2 Ride **straight** toward Lewis and Clark State Park.

17.4 Turn **right** into **Lewis and Clark Park**. Enjoy the park (picnic areas, restrooms, water) and then retrace your route out the park, turning **left** on the **Scenic Highway**.

17.7 Turn **right** over the Sandy River Bridge and into Troutdale. The road becomes **Columbia Boulevard** through Troutdale.

18.1 Harlow House Museum on your left.

18.6 Turn **right** toward Interstate 84 on **Graham Road** (unmarked). Follow the signs marking the 40-Mile Loop all the way to Blue Lake Park.

19.0 Turn **left** toward Marine Drive on **Frontage Road** (unmarked).

19.3 Turn **right** to **Marine Drive**.

20.1 The bike route crosses to the other side of Marine Drive and is a separated path here.

22.1 The bike path intersects with **Blue Lake Road**, turn **left**.

22.5 Turn **right** into **Blue Lake Park**. Enjoy the swimming, boating, picnicking, and game fields in this popular park. To continue the ride, follow back turning **left** from the park, heading back to Marine Drive.

23.3 Turn **left** on **Marine Drive**. Follow the bike route, including the off-road bike path along the river.

28.3 Cross Marine Drive to get on the **I-205 bike path** heading south toward Columbia Boulevard.

29.5 Cross Columbia Boulevard, following the bike route signs.

33.2 Turn **right** from the bike path to **Yamhill Street.**

34.2 Four-way stop sign at **76th Avenue**, turn **right** and then **left** to stay on **Yamhill**.

34.6 Turn **left** at **69th Avenue** and ride one block to return to **Mt. Tabor Park**.

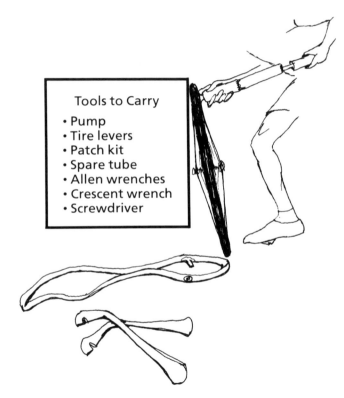

Tools to Carry

- Pump
- Tire levers
- Patch kit
- Spare tube
- Allen wrenches
- Crescent wrench
- Screwdriver

11 Tualatin River

34 miles
from West Linn
moderate

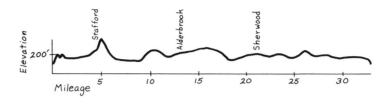

Despite urban sprawl, there are still many miles of good bicycling in the Tualatin River valley. This ride over mildly hilly terrain takes you through some pleasant scenery and down some delightful stretches. While the Tualatin River is not seen for most of the ride, it's interesting to compare its gorge at the starting point with its flat quiet waters seen from Elsner Road.

0.0 Start at **Willamette Park** in West Linn, at the foot of 12th Street on the Willamette River. Begin by riding up 12th Street.

0.4 Stop sign at **7th Avenue**, turn **right**.

0.5 Turn **left** on **10th Street**, and go under the freeway.

0.8 T-intersection at **Blankenship Road**/Salamo Road, turn **left** on Blankenship.

1.2 Turn **left** with **Blankenship** at the Debok Street intersection.

1.4 Turn **right** on **Johnson Road**.

4.7 T-intersection at **Stafford Road**, turn **right** (Stafford is sometimes busy).

5.0 Turn **left** on **Childs Road**.

6.5 Turn **right** on **Bryant Road**.

7.9 Four-way stop at **Lakeview Boulevard**, turn **right**.

8.9 Curve **left** with **Lakeview**.

9.1 T-intersection at **Iron Mountain Boulevard/Upper Drive**, turn **left**.

9.8 Stop sign at **Reese Road**, turn **right**.

10.0 Cross Boones Ferry Road and continue on **Oak Ridge Road**.

10.4 Turn **right** on **Waluga Drive**.

10.8 Cross Carman Drive, and the road becomes **Bonita Road**.

12.5 T-intersection at **Hall Boulevard**, turn **left**.

12.5 Turn **right** on **Pinebrook Street**.

12.9 T-intersection at **92nd Avenue**, turn **left**. This becomes **Alderbrook Drive**.

13.2 Alderbrook Drive turns **right**. Follow Alderbrook Drive carefully without getting mistaken by the Lanes, Roads, and Circles.

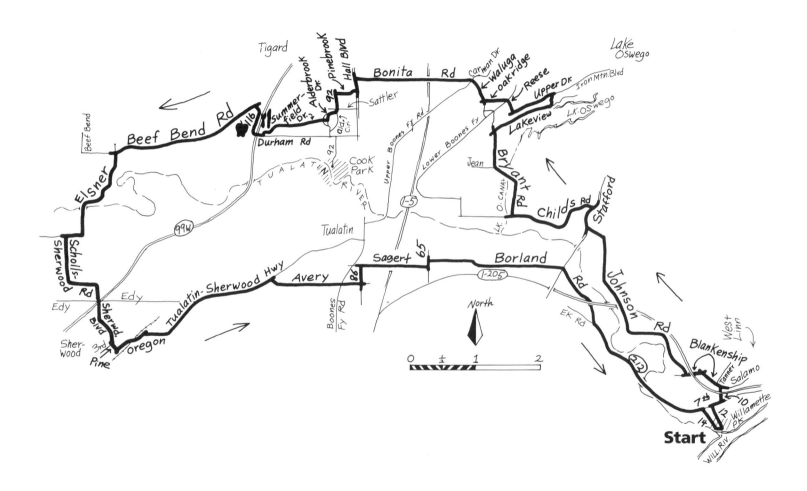

13.5 Turn **right** on **Summerfield Drive** (not Lane).

14.6 T-intersection at **Durham Road**, turn **right**, and cross Highway 99.

14.7 The road curves right and becomes **116th Avenue**.

15.2 T-intersection at **Beef Bend Road**, turn **left**.

17.7 Turn **left** on **Elsner Road** (in the middle of a downhill run, so watch for the sign).

19.5 T-intersection at **Scholls-Sherwood Road**, turn **left**.

21.0 Stop sign at **Edy Road**, turn **left** and cross Highway 99.

21.0 T-intersection, turn **right** on **Sherwood Boulevard**.

21.8 Turn **left** on **Pine Street**.

21.9 Turn **left** on **Oregon Street**. This becomes **Tualatin-Sherwood Road** where traffic can be busy on weekdays.

24.8 Turn **right** on **Avery Street**.

26.2 Four-way stop sign at **86th Avenue**, turn **left**.

26.4 T-intersection at **Sagert Street**, turn **right**.

27.5 Stop sign at **65th Avenue**, turn **left**.

27.6 Stop sign at **Borland Road**, turn **right**. This becomes **7th Avenue** in West Linn.

33.2 Turn **right** on **14th Street**, and go downhill into the park.

33.6 Return to **Willamette Park** on the river.

12 Vancouver Lake

32 miles
from north Portland
moderate

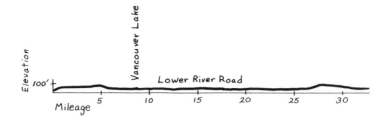

This flat, water-oriented ride takes you to Vancouver Lake Park, a large well-kept picnic area, where you can swim, watch sailboats, search the marshes for birds or amphibians, or just enjoy the placid expanse of the lake.

Lower River Road goes through an area of farms, then runs along the Columbia River, becoming at its north end a small lane a few feet from the shoreline. You're sure to see cows, a great blue heron, and a friendly wave from one of the local people.

0.0 Meet in Portland's **East Delta Park** near the restrooms by the playing fields. Head north and east as the road winds under Highway 99.
0.3 Turn **left** at **Vancouver Way**.
0.3 T-intersection at **Marine Drive**, turn **left**.
0.4 Turn **right** with the **bike route**, avoiding the freeway entrance.
0.6 Cross **left** onto the **bike route** and follow the signs, taking you over various sidewalks, street crossings and through a tunnel.
1.7 The bike route uses the bridge sidewalk to cross the Columbia River.
2.4 The bike route ends at a T-intersection at **Columbia Street**, turn **right**.
2.7 Traffic light at **8th Street**, turn **left**.
2.9 Turn **right** on **Franklin Street**.
3.1 Stop sign at **13th Street**, turn **left**.
3.3 Turn **right** on **Kauffman Avenue**.
4.0 Traffic light at **Fourth Plain Boulevard**, turn **left**.
4.5 Merge left to stay on Fourth Plain Boulevard.
7.9 Continue **straight** following the sign for Vancouver Lake.
8.6 Turn **right** into **Vancouver Lake Park**. There are restrooms, drinking water, swimming, sailboards, and views of Mt. Hood, some of which are available only during the warmer season. After enjoying the park, ride back the way you came.
9.2 Stop sign at Lower River Road (unmarked), turn **right**.
16.5 The road ends; turn around, and notice the wind direction.
23.9 The road curves **right** onto River Road (unmarked). This becomes Fourth Plain Boulevard.

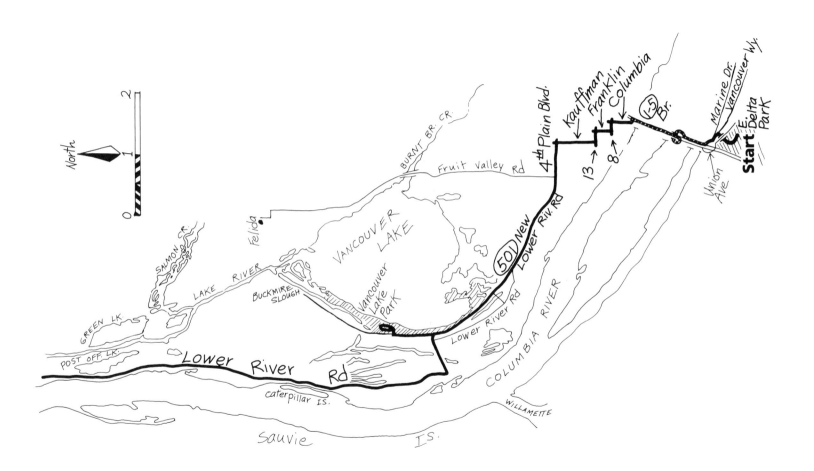

North

2
1
0

BURNT BR. CR.

Fruit Valley Rd.

4th Plain Blvd.

Kauffman

Franklin

Columbia

I-5 Br.

Marine Dr.

Vancouver Wy.

Start E. Delta Park

13 →

8 →

Union Ave.

501 New Lower Riv. Rd.

VANCOUVER LAKE

Felida

Vancouver Lake Park

SALMON CR.

LAKE RIVER

BUCKMIRE SLOUGH

GREEN LK.

POST OFF. LK.

Lower River Rd

Lower River Rd

COLUMBIA RIVER

caterpillar IS.

WILLAMETTE

SAUVIE IS.

27.9 Traffic light at **Kauffman Avenue**, turn **right**.
28.5 T-intersection at **13th Street**, turn **left**.
28.7 Turn **right** on **Franklin Street**.
29.0 T-intersection at **8th Avenue**, turn **left**.
29.1 Traffic light at **Columbia Street** by Esther Short Park, turn **right**.
29.4 Turn **left** onto the **bike route** just after riding under a railroad bridge. Follow the bike route over the bridge and back toward Delta Park.
31.9 Return to the starting point in **East Delta Park**.

13 Wheatland Ferry

50 miles
from Champoeg Park, south of Wilsonville
moderate

Although one could easily fill two or three days cycling through the relaxed flat French Prairie area, these 50 miles make up a representative route and take you to a few points not to be missed. The Wheatland Ferry is one of the few remaining public ferries crossing the Willamette River. Several fruit stands greet you along the way. And the state parks—Maud Williamson and Willamette Mission—are quiet peaceful settings typical of the Willamette Valley countryside.

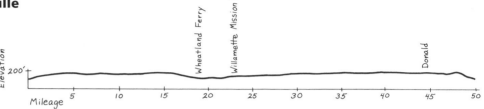

0.0 Start at the Visitor Center in **Champoeg Park** (ride there using the Champoeg Park ride, or drive there taking Exit 278 from the I-5 freeway). Head west (turn right) out of the park on Champoeg Road.
0.3 Turn **left** on **French Prairie Road**.
3.8 Intersection with **St. Paul Highway, Ore. 219**, turn **right**.
5.8 Town of St. Paul. Turn **left** toward Fairfield on **River Road**.
13.8 T-intersection at **French Prairie Road**, which is **Ore. 219** here. Turn **right** toward Wheatland.
15.5 Turn **right** on **Matheny Road**.
18.7 Turn **right**, keeping on **Matheny Road**.
19.2 Wheatland Ferry landing. Take your bike across the river, free crossing for bicycles.
20.4 Cross Highway 221 (Dayton-Salem Highway) to enter Maud Williamson State Park. Relax, then turn around to take the ferry back.
22.4 T-intersection at **Wheatland Road**, turn **right**.
23.2 Willamette Mission State Park on the right.
24.1 Turn **left** on **Waconda Road**.
32.3 T-intersection at **Howell-Prairie Road**, turn **left**.
33.8 Turn **left** on **Mt. Angel-Gervais Road**.

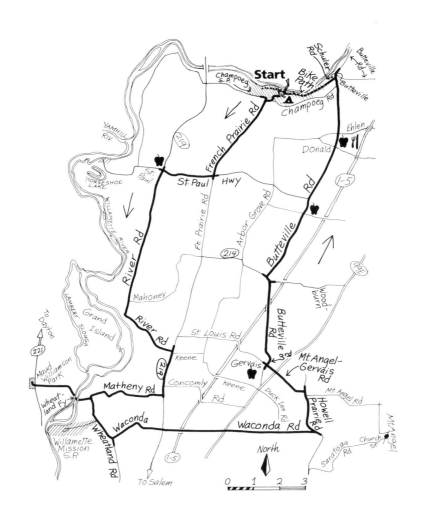

42 Wheatland Ferry

35.7 Town of Gervais. Turn **right** on **3rd Street**, toward Donald. This road becomes Butteville Road.

39.0 T-intersection at **Ore. 214**, turn **left**.

39.2 Turn **right** to Donald, on **Butteville Road**.

42.0 Town of Broadacres.

44.8 Town of Donald. Town hub is two blocks to the right.

47.4 Turn **left** on **Schuler Road** to the bike path.

47.8 Turn **left** onto the **bike path** through Champoeg Park. This path winds through the woods on the north flank of the hill La Butte.

49.7 Turn **right** on the road, and follow the bike path to the Visitor Center.

50.2 Turn **left** across the road on the bike path and cross the creek.

50.4 Return to the Visitor Center.

14 Willamette River

23 miles
from southwest Portland
moderate

This ride takes you from Sellwood to Oregon City and back, mostly on designated bicycle routes, and lends itself to a leisurely pace with time to stop and look or explore. If you've ever wanted to go out to one of those islands in the river, for instance, you can take the short trail to Elk Rock Island, which is accessible during low water periods. Good river views and parks recur throughout the ride, which concludes by winding uphill through wooded Tryon Creek Park for a thrilling descent down Taylors Ferry Road.

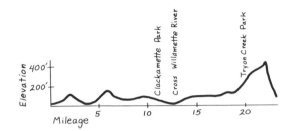

0.0 Start in Portland's **Willamette Park** on the river at S.W. Nebraska Street by Macadam Avenue. Ride to the south end of the park on the bike path.

0.4 Go out of the park onto **Miles Place**, which turns into a bike path.

0.6 Take the **right fork** of the path.

0.7 At busy Macadam Avenue, don't cross it, but turn **left** onto the **sidewalk**.

0.9 Turn **left** at the Staff Jennings sign, then **right** to follow the bike route across the Sellwood Bridge.

1.5 Turn **left** on **6th Avenue** for one block.

1.5 Turn **right** on **Spokane Street**.

1.8 Stop sign at **13th Avenue**, turn **right**.

2.4 Cross the railroad tracks; the road becomes **Exeter Drive**, then **St. Andrews Drive**.

2.8 Stop sign at **17th Avenue**, turn **right** (this is also called River Road).

3.7 Traffic light at **McLoughlin Boulevard**, continue riding south using the sidewalk if desired.

4.0 Traffic light at the entrance to the Kellogg Creek Plant, turn **right** and follow the driveway past the official signs, to the bike path on the river.

4.3 Bike path turns onto **19th Avenue**.

4.4 Turn **left** with the bike route onto **Bluebird Street**. Or, to visit Elk Rock Island, follow 19th Avenue till it ends at Sparrow Street. Park your bike and follow the path out to the island.

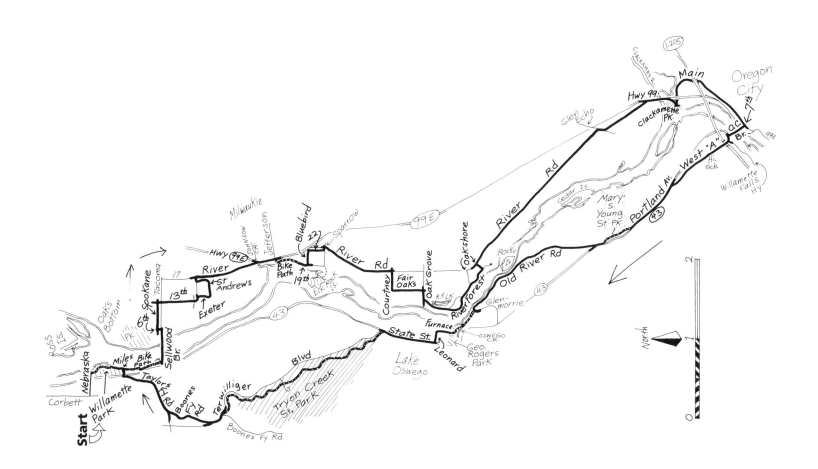

4.6 Turn **right** on 22nd Avenue, following the bike route.

4.8 Continue on the bike route now on **River Road**.

5.7 Flashing yellow light at **Courtney Road**, turn **right**. This curves left and becomes Fair Oaks Avenue.

6.4 Stop sign at **Oak Grove Boulevard**, turn **right**.

6.5 Turn **left** to **River Forest Drive**. This becomes River Forest Court.

7.2 T-intersection at **River Forest Road**, turn **right**. This becomes River Forest Place.

7.7 Turn **left** on **Oak Shore Lane**.

7.8 T-intersection on **River Road**, turn **right**.

10.2 Curve **right** with the bike route at **Glen Echo Avenue**, then **left** on **River Road**.

10.9 Stop sign at **McLoughlin Boulevard**, use the **sidewalk** and cross the bridge.

11.1 Turn **right** at the first off-ramp.

11.2 Stop sign at **Main Street**. Clackamette Park is to the right, with picnicking, river views, restrooms. To continue, turn **left** under the overpass.

12.6 Traffic light at **7th Street**, turn **right** onto the Oregon City Bridge.

12.8 Turn **left** following the signs to the High School, up the hill (Willamette Falls Boulevard).

12.9 Turn **right** on **West A Street**.

13.9 Stop sign on **Portland Avenue**, turn **left**.

14.7 Take the separated bike path along Mary S. Young Park. Or, turn into the park for paths, river access, picnicking, restrooms.

15.2 Turn **right** as the sign marks "Alternative Bike Route" (Old River Road).

17.1 Where the road curves left and uphill, go **right** taking the **bike path** across the creek.

17.4 Turn **right** across the bridge, into Rogers Park.

17.5 Turn **right** at the fork on **Furnace Street**.

17.8 Turn **left** on **Leonard Street**.

17.9 Stop sign at **State Street**, turn **right**. This is a busy street, but there is no good alternative.

18.6 Turn **left** on **Terwilliger Boulevard**, and use the bike path.

20.1 Turn **right** on the path toward Lewis and Clark. Or, to see the Tryon Creek Nature House keep straight.

21.3 Where the park ends at Boones Ferry Road, cross Terwilliger and continue north on Terwilliger.

21.4 Turn **right** on **Boones Ferry Road**.

22.1 Stop sign at **Taylors Ferry Road**, turn **right**.

22.9 Traffic signal at Macadam Avenue, go straight, and the road is called Miles Street.

23.0 T-intersection at **Miles Place**, turn **left**.

23.4 Return to the starting point in **Willamette Park** at Nebraska Street.

Bike Routes

There are lots of ways road engineers design bike routes. One is the bike path, a separated route off the road. Then there's the bike lane, where the shoulder is designated for bicycles. Sometimes a street is labeled Bike Route, meaning the street is recommended for bicycle traffic, and bikes usually share the road with cars.

The art and science of developing bike routes are still evolving, and some bike routes have proven less safe than others. For instance, if the bike route is filled with joggers, skateboarders, dogs and their owners, and you're coasting down hill at 20 miles per hour, it may be safer to cycle in the roadway. Another example is the shoulder bike lane on only one side of the street, which is safe for cyclists going the same direction as cars on that side of the street, but dangerous for cyclists going the other way. Never ride against traffic, even in a shoulder bike lane.

As bike routes are being designed, it's important for cyclists to inform the engineers about what designs are safe and comfortable.

15 Winery Tour

39 miles
from southwest Portland
moderate

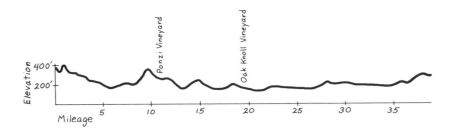

Visiting the two wineries along this route is really just an excuse to go on a nice bike ride in the country. The route begins by winding through a park-like neighborhood in southwest Portland, travels country roads enlivened by occasional short hills, and brings you back on some of the Beaverton area's bicycle routes.

Oak Knoll Winery, midway along the route, has picnic tables on the grounds. Both vineyards give short tours; call ahead for scheduling if you plan on this.

0.0 From **Gabriel Park**, S.W. 45th and Vermont Street in Portland, begin by going south on 45th Avenue.

0.6 Traffic signal at Multnomah Boulevard, turn a **sharp right** onto **Maplewood Road**, which becomes 52nd Avenue.

1.3 Stop sign at **Nevada Court**, turn **left**.

1.7 T-intersection at **60th Avenue**, turn **left**.

2.0 The road curves right and becomes **Canby Street**.

2.5 Turn **left** on **68th Avenue**.

2.7 Stop sign at **Garden Home Road**, turn **right**.

2.8 Turn **left** on **71st Avenue**.

3.2 The road curves right and becomes **Alden Street**.

3.6 T-intersection at **80th Avenue**, turn **left**.

4.8 Stop sign at **Oak Street**, turn **right**.

5.7 T-intersection at **Greenburg Road**. **Cross Oak Street** (left) using the pedestrian signal, then **cross Greenburg Road**, also using the pedestrian signal. (Vehicle left turn is illegal.) Go **left** (south) on **Greenburg**, using the sidewalk.

5.9 Turn **right** on **Cascade Avenue**.

6.7 T-intersection at **Scholls Ferry Road** (Highway 210), turn **left**.

8.4 Go **straight** onto **Old Scholls Ferry Road** (marked "To Murray Boulevard").

10.3 Stop sign at **Scholls Ferry Road**, turn **right**.

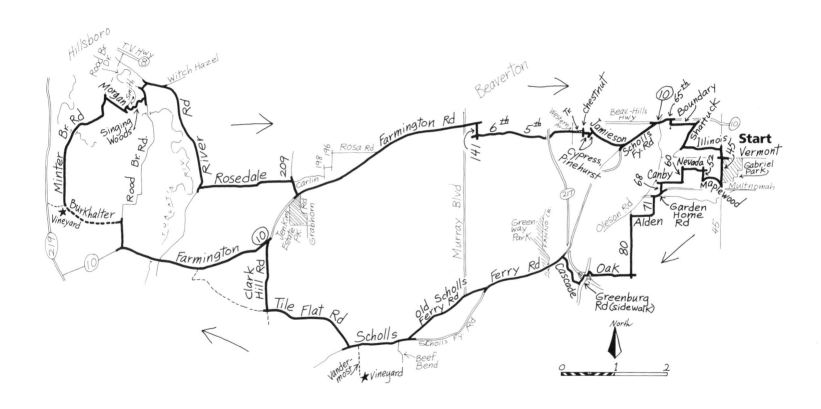

11.3 To visit Ponzi Vineyards, turn left on Vandermost Road, a one-mile unpaved road. This side trip is not included in the mileage.

11.5 Turn **right** on **Tile Flat Road**.

13.5 Turn **right** on **Clark Hill Road**.

14.9 T-intersection at **Highway 10** (Farmington Road), turn **left**.

18.0 Turn **right** on **Rood Bridge Road**.

18.6 Turn **left** on **Burkhalter Road** to Oak Knoll Vineyards. Burkhalter is unpaved but rideable; if you don't want to visit this winery or ride on Burkhalter, follow Rood Bridge Road to River Road.

19.6 Oak Knoll Vineyards, end of unpaved section.

19.9 Road curves right and becomes **Minter Bridge Road**.

22.4 Turn **right** on **Morgan Road**.

22.9 Turn **left** on **Singing Woods Drive**, and follow the signs carefully since Singing Woods curves unpredictably.

23.5 Stop sign at **Rood Bridge Road**, turn **left**.

23.9 Traffic signal at **River Road**, turn **right**.

26.4 Turn **left** on **Rosedale Road**.

28.4 Stop sign at **209th Avenue**, turn **right**.

28.6 T-intersection at **Highway 10** (Farmington Road), turn **left**.

32.5 Turn **right** on **141st Avenue** (two blocks past Murray Boulevard).

32.8 Turn **left** on **6th Street** (Beaverton Bike Route #20). Sixth Street curves into **5th Street**.

35.0 5th Street ends, continue on the **bike trail**.

35.0 Turn **right** on **Chestnut Place** for 1/2 block.

35.0 Stop sign at **Cypress Street**, turn **left** (still Bike Route #20).

35.3 Jog **left** on **Pinehurst Drive**.

35.3 T-intersection at **Jamieson Road**, turn **right**.

36.0 T-intersection at **Scholls Ferry Road**, turn **left**.

36.8 Traffic signal at **Beaverton-Hillsdale Highway**, turn **right**, being careful of the traffic here.

37.1 Turn **right** on **65th Avenue** for one block.

37.2 Turn **left** on **Boundary Street**.

37.7 Stop sign at **Shattuck Road**, turn **right**.

38.2 Turn **left** on **Illinois Street** (across from the entrance to the Alpenrose Velodrome).

39.0 T-intersection at **45th Avenue**, turn **right**.

39.1 Return to **Gabriel Park**, S.W. 45th and Vermont Street.

Bike Camping

For many of us biking enthusiasts, a one-day ride is not enough. The joys of being away with your bike on an overnight trip are heightened to new dimensions as you feel the expansion in your sense of self-sufficiency, your strength, your self-confidence, and your well-being.

The five overnight routes collected in this book (appearing at the end of the Moderate Rides, Challenging Rides, and Most Difficult Rides) are ideal for a first-time bike camper as well as the experienced tourist who wants a quick get-away.

If you haven't done any bike camping, check with your cycling friends or with bike shop employees about what to take and how to do it; there are lots of styles of bike touring. Then take off on a wonderful adventure with one of these tours.

16 Champoeg Park

Campground for overnight
Day 1: 34 miles
Day 2: 24 miles
from Lake Oswego
moderate

A bike camping trip to Champoeg Park could be just an overnight stop, or it could be the opportunity to explore the whole French Prairie area by bicycle, using the park as your home-away-from-home. Either way, this loop is an easy way to take a bicycle vacation.

The trip from Portland to Champoeg takes you by open farm lands, rolling hills, kid goats and calves, and the Willamette River bank. The return trip presents bike paths, views of Mt. Hood, strengthening climbs and thrilling descents—and most of it on quiet country roads, ideal for cycling.

Champoeg is a large state park along the Willamette River, with a museum and information center. The campground (open year round) offers camping sites that fit motorized recreation vehicles, and a large hiker/biker area for tents.

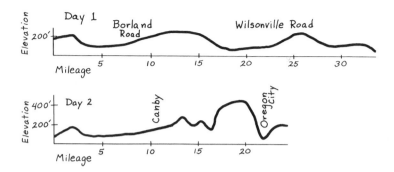

Day 1

0.0 This trip begins at **Mary S. Young Park** on Highway 43 between Lake Oswego and West Linn. Head south on the highway (**left** when you leave the park) toward West Linn. Follow the bike route.

1.6 Turn **right** on **West A Avenue**.

2.5 Stop sign at **Willamette Falls Drive**, turn **right**.

2.7 Fork in the road, take the **left** fork to stay on Willamette Falls Drive.

2.9 West Linn. Continue straight. The road is called **7th Avenue**, and then **Borland Road**.

6.3 Cross the Tualatin River.

7.4 Curve right, staying on Borland Road.

8.5 Cross Stafford Road.

10.6 T-intersection at **65th Avenue**, turn **left**.

10.7 Turn **right** on **Sagert Street**.

11.8 Stop sign at **Boones Ferry Road**, turn **left**.

12.9 Turn **right** on **Graham's Ferry Road**. It soon curves left.

14.6 Curve **right** as Graham's Ferry Road curves.

17.9 Cross Bell Road and continue on Graham's Ferry Road.

18.7 Stop sign at **Wilsonville Road,** go **straight**.

28.1 T-intersection at **Highway 219**, turn **left** toward Champoeg.

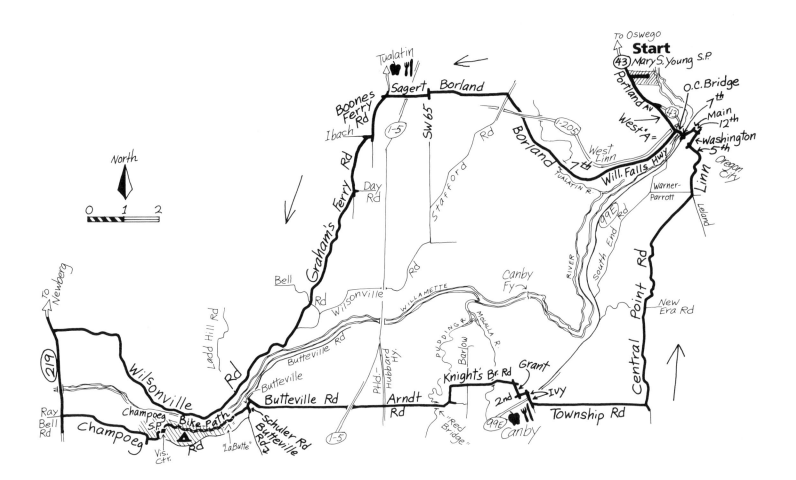

North

0 1 2

To Oswego

Start

43 Mary S. Young S.P.

Portland Av

O.C. Bridge

7th
Main
12th

West "A"

Washington
5th

West Linn

7th

Will. Falls Hwy

Oregon City

Linn

Leland

Warner-Parrott

Tualatin

Sagert   Borland

Boones Ferry Rd

Ibach Rd

I-5

SW 65

Graham's Ferry Rd

Day Rd

Stafford Rd

I-205

Borland

Tualatin R.

99 E

South End Rd

RIVER

Central Point Rd

New Era Rd

Bell

Rd

Ladd Hill Rd

Rd

Wilsonville Rd

WILLAMETTE

Canby Fy

219

To Newberg

Wilsonville

Butteville Rd

Butteville

Butteville Rd

Champoeg S.P.

Bike Path

Ray Bell Rd

Champoeg

Vis. Ctr.

"LaButte"

Schuler Rd
Butteville Rd

Arndt Rd

I-5

Phd.

Hubbard Hy.

PUDDING R.

Barlow

MOLALLA R.

Knight's Br. Rd

"Red Bridge"

Grant

2nd   Ivy

99 E   Canby

Township Rd

29.7 Cross the Willamette River.
30.4 Turn **left** on **Champoeg Road** (unlabeled) toward Champoeg.
32.8 Champoeg Road curves left.
33.0 Turn **left** into Champoeg Park, and follow the bike path to the campground.
33.8 Campground.

Day 2

0.0 Leave Champoeg campground, turning **right** just past the registration building, following the **bike path**.
1.8 Bike path ends, continue **straight** on narrow road.
2.2 T-intersection at **Butteville Road** (unmarked), turn **left**.
2.4 Road curves right, becomes **Arndt Road**.
7.6 Turn **left** on **Knight's Bridge Road**.
9.8 Stop sign at **Grant Street**, turn **right**.
10.1 Stop sign at **2nd Avenue**, turn **left**.
10.3 Stop sign at **Ivy Street**, turn **right**.
10.6 Turn **left** on **Township Road**.
13.6 Stop sign at **Central Point Road**, turn **left**.
19.7 Four-way stop sign at **Linn Avenue**, turn **left**. This curves down a hill, turns and becomes **5th Street**.
21.2 Traffic light at **Washington Street**, turn **right**.
21.7 Flashing light at **12th Street**, turn **left**.
21.8 Stop sign at **Main Street**, turn **left**.
22.1 Traffic light on **7th Street**, turn **right** and cross the bridge over the Willamette River.
22.3 Turn **left** following the signs to the **High School**.
22.4 Turn **right** on **West A Street**, again following the sign to the High School.
23.3 T-intersection at **Portland Avenue**, turn **left**.
24.4 Turn **right** into **Mary S. Young Park**.

17 Oxbow Park

**Campground for overnight
19 miles each day
from southeast Portland
moderate**

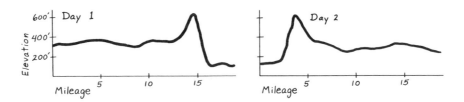

Oxbow Park is close enough that you can decide in the afternoon that you want to go camping and pack your bike and ride there before the sun goes down.

The park is a beautiful treed expanse along the Sandy River, full of hiking trails, deer, river views, and relaxation. And the ride to Oxbow is along woods, creeks, and farmlands, once you're past the city developments. There is a steep one-mile hill just before the park—down hill going there and up hill coming back.

Oxbow Park, open year round, is maintained and operated by Multnomah County. Camping fees are collected in the Park. On a hot summer weekend the campsites fill up, so plan to arrive early. Or choose to come here during those clear days in September when it isn't crowded and the park shows its autumn colors.

Day 1

0.0 Lents Park in Portland is the beginning point in this tour, S.E. 88th and Holgate Boulevard. Ride east on Holgate.

0.2 After crossing 92nd Avenue but before crossing over the I-205 freeway, turn **left** on the **bike path**.

1.3 Turn **right** on **Division Street**.

12.4 Curve **right** on **Oxbow Drive**, toward Oxbow Park.

13.8 Curve **left** on **Oxbow Drive**, toward Oxbow Park.

14.6 Turn **left** on **Oxbow Parkway** toward Oxbow Park campsites.

16.3 Park entrance.

18.8 Follow sign into campground.

Day 2

0.0 Leave the campground, heading back through the park.

3.9 Stop sign at **Oxbow Drive**, turn **right**. This turns into Division Street.

17.2 After riding under the I-205 overpass, then over the ramp underpass, turn **left** onto the **bike path**.

18.3 Turn **right** on **Holgate Boulevard**.

18.6 Lents Park, 88th and Holgate.

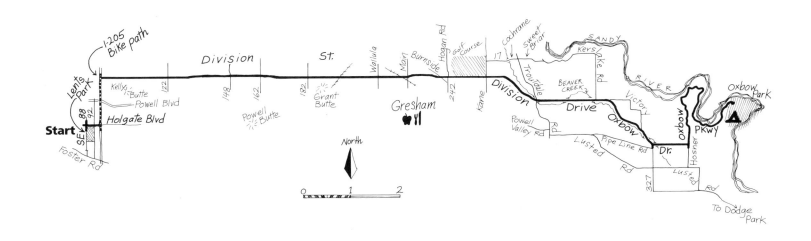

I-205
Bike path

Lents
Park

Division   St.

Kelly
Butte
Powell Blvd

Holgate Blvd

Start

SE

88
92

Foster
Rd

122

148

162

182

Grant
Butte

Powell
Butte

Walula

Marr

Burnside

Hogan Rd

Golf
Course

Gresham

242

Kane

17

Cochrane

Sweet
Briar

Troutdale

Division

Drive

Oxbow

Beaver
Creek

Kers
Lake Rd

Victory

SANDY

RIVER

Oxbow
Park

Oxbow

PKWY

Powell
Valley Rd

Lusted

Rd

Pipe Line Rd

Dr.

Hosner

Lusted

Rd

327

To Dodge
Park

North

0   1   2

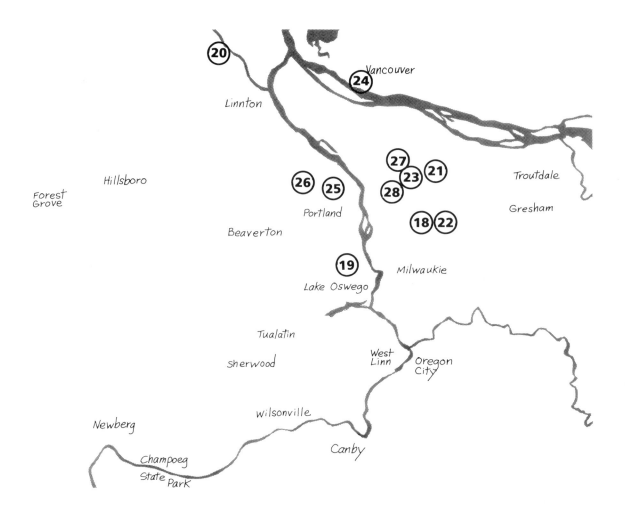

Forest Grove

Hillsboro

Linnton

(20)

Vancouver (24)

Troutdale

(27)
(23) (21)
(28)

Gresham

(26) (25)

Portland

Beaverton

(18) (22)

(19)

Lake Oswego

Milwaukie

Tualatin

Sherwood

West Linn

Oregon City

Wilsonville

Newberg

Champoeg State Park

Canby

Challenging Rides

18 Bertha's Birthday Ride

29 miles
from southeast Portland
challenging

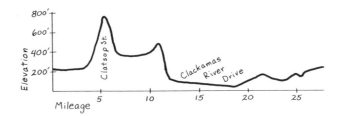

When Anndy's bike, named Bertha, was ten years old, she invited several of her bicycle friends to celebrate with a Birthday Ride, which went along this route. Since then, no other name would stay with this ride through Pleasant Valley and along the Clackamas River, so we still call it Bertha's Birthday Ride. And we encourage other bicycles (and cyclists) to celebrate with birthday rides!

0.0 Begin at **Mt. Scott Park** in Portland, S.E. 72nd and Harold Street. Head south on 72nd Avenue.
0.2 Traffic signal at **Woodstock Boulevard**, turn **left**.
1.2 Traffic signal at **92nd Avenue**, turn **left**.
1.5 Traffic signal at **Harold Street**, turn **right**.
3.2 Stop sign at **128th Avenue**, turn **right**.
3.7 Stop sign at **Foster Road**, turn **left**.
4.0 Turn **right** on **134th Avenue**. This street becomes **Deardorf Road**, and takes you over Johnson Creek and up the hill toward Happy Valley. Many cyclists ponder this name while climbing in their 28-inch low gear.
5.3 Turn **left** on **Clatsop Street**.
6.8 T-intersection at **162nd Avenue**, turn **left**.
6.9 Turn **right** on **Baxter Road**.
7.3 T-intersection at **170th Avenue**, turn **right**.
7.5 Stop sign at **172nd Avenue**, turn **right**.
10.8 T-intersection at **Armstrong Circle**, turn **left**.
11.2 T-intersection at **Highway 212**, turn **left**.
11.3 Turn **right** on **Tong Road**.
12.5 T-intersection at **Highway 224**, turn **right**.
13.5 Town of Carver. Turn **left** following the sign "To Redland" and cross the bridge over the Clackamas River.
13.7 Turn **right** onto **Clackamas River Drive**, which follows the river downstream for several miles.

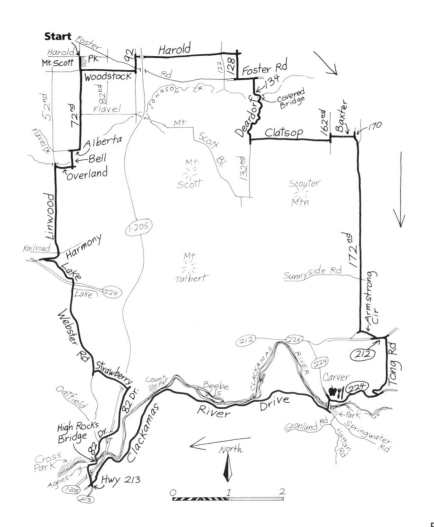

19.3 Traffic signal at **Highway 213**, turn **right**, toward Portland, and cross the I-205 Freeway.

19.8 Turn **left** onto the **bike path** bridge over the Clackamas River. Cross Park is just on the north side of the river.

19.9 Continue on **82nd Drive**. Use caution around the freeway entrance.

21.4 Turn **left** on **Strawberry Lane**.

22.1 T-intersection at **Webster Road**, turn **right**.

23.8 Cross Highway 224 and the road is called **Lake Road**.

24.5 Traffic light at **Harmony Road**, turn **right**. This becomes Linwood Avenue.

26.3 Turn **right** on **Overland Road**.

26.6 Stop sign at **Bell Avenue**, turn **left**.

26.9 T-intersection at **Alberta Avenue**, turn **right**. This turns into **72nd Avenue**.

28.7 Return to **Mt. Scott Park** at 72nd and Harold Street.

19 Canby Ferry

39 miles
from southwest Portland
challenging

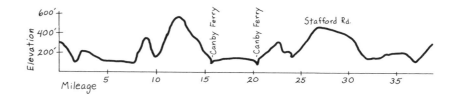

The Canby Ferry is a favorite bike ride from Portland, and its popularity is well deserved. You travel along the Terwilliger bike path, through quiet farmlands to spacious views, and of course to the Canby Ferry. The ferry ride itself has its pleasures: the calm relaxed spot in the river, the hum of the ferry carrying you across the water, and the warm smile on the ferry operator's face.

This variation from the more commonly ridden direct route (from Lake Oswego up McVey and Stafford Roads) presents more interesting scenery and easier traffic, although there are still short sections where it's busy.

0.0 Start at **Tryon Creek State Park**, on S.W. Terwilliger Boulevard, south of Boones Ferry Road in Portland. Head south on the bike path toward Lake Oswego.
1.5 Bike path ends on Macadam Avenue, called State Street in Lake Oswego. Turn **right**.
1.8 Traffic signal at **B Avenue**, turn **right**.
2.3 Stop sign at **Eighth Street**, turn **left**.
2.5 T-intersection at **Evergreen Road**, turn **right**.
2.6 T-intersection at **Tenth Street**, turn **left**.
2.6 Bear **right** on **Berwick Road**.
2.8 T-intersection at **Iron Mountain Boulevard**, turn **left**.
4.2 Turn **left** to **Lakeview Boulevard**.
6.0 T-intersection at **Pilkington Road**, turn **left**.
6.1 Stop sign at **Jean Road**, turn **left**.
6.7 T-intersection at **Bryant Road**, turn **right**.
7.5 T-intersection at **Childs Road**, turn **left**.
9.0 T-intersection at **Stafford Road**, turn **right**.
11.4 Turn **left** on **Mountain Road**.
15.6 T-intersection, turn **left** to the Canby Ferry. Beware of the speed bumps that have caused several bike accidents.
15.8 Ride the free ferry across the Willamette River.
16.1 Road curves right and becomes 37th Avenue.
16.3 Molalla River State Park is to the right. Good picnicking, hiking, relaxing, river viewing. 37th Avenue then curves left becoming Holly Street.

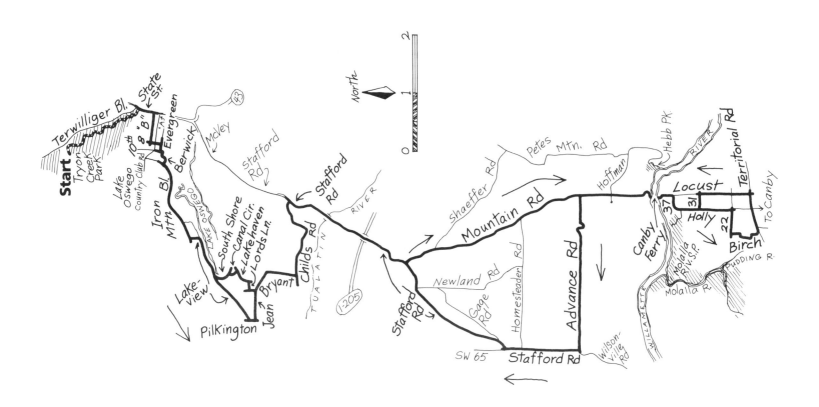

17.2 Turn **right** on **22nd Avenue**.

17.6 Turn **left** on **Birch Street**, through acres of dahlia fields. The dahlias are at their best July through September.

18.2 Birch Street curves **left** onto **Territorial Road**.

18.8 Turn **left** on **Locust Street**. Locust shortly curves **left** to 31st Avenue.

19.9 T-intersection at **Holly Street**, turn **right**.

20.8 Ferry crossing.

22.6 Turn **left** on **Advance Road**, toward Wilsonville.

24.8 Turn **right** on **Stafford Road** toward Oregon City.

30.7 Turn **left** on **Childs Road**.

32.1 Turn **right** on **Bryant Road**, toward Lake Grove.

33.2 Turn **right** on **Lords Lane**, which becomes Lake Haven Drive.

33.6 Turn **left** on **Canal Circle**.

33.7 Stop sign at **South Shore Boulevard**, go **straight**.

33.9 T-intersection at **Lakeview Boulevard**, turn **right**.

34.8 T-intersection at **Iron Mountain Boulevard**, turn **right**.

36.2 Turn **right** on **Berwick Road**.

36.3 Bear **left** to **Tenth Street**.

36.4 Turn **right** to **Evergreen Street**.

36.5 Turn **left** to **Eighth Street**.

36.7 Stop sign at **B Avenue**, turn **right**.

37.2 Traffic signal at **State Street**, turn **left**.

37.5 Turn **left** on **Terwilliger Boulevard** and ride up the bike path.

39.0 Return to **Tryon Creek State Park**.

The Canby Ferry began operating in 1914, when the roads were traveled by horses and carts. Today's ferry carries up to five cars or dozens of bicyclists for the four-minute crossing, free for cyclists. The Canby Ferry operates 6:45 am till 9:00 pm, but is closed when the river is high or when work is being done. Call the Clackamas County Road Department, 655-8521, to find out if the ferry is running.

20 Crossing the Tualatin Mountains

22 miles
from Highway 30 at Logie Trail Road
challenging

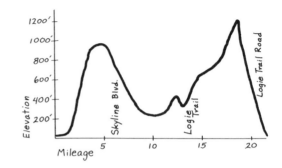

The Tualatin Mountains separate the Columbia River from the valley farmlands to the southwest. This route takes you across two of the mountain passes and enables you to see quite different terrain in just 22 miles.

These few miles include some of the hardest miles in the area. Any road that leads you up to Skyline is an admirable climb, but cycling up Mc-Namee Road gains you special respect (you'll see why). The second summit is a grandiose 1230 feet above sea level, and then you shoot down to the Columbia River level in just 2½ miles.

In between the climbs is a relaxing rural stretch with farms, apple trees, an old church, and the ubiquitous cows of rural life.

A word of caution for the unadventurous: one mile of Logie Trail Road is not paved, but rideable.

0.0 Begin on **Highway 30** at **Logie Trail Road** northwest of Portland. Ride east on Highway 30.
1.2 Turn **right** on **McNamee Road**, and go up the hill.
5.8 T-intersection at **Skyline Boulevard**, turn **right**.
7.3 Stop sign at Cornelius Pass Road. Cross the road to **Old Cornelius Pass Road** and turn **left**.
9.0 Stop sign at **Phillips Road**, turn **right**.
11.3 T-intersection at **Helvetia Road**, turn **right**.
13.4 Turn **right** on **Logie Trail Road**.
14.7 Road becomes gravel.
15.9 Road is paved. Logie Trail becomes Johnson Road.
18.3 Summit at **Skyline Boulevard**, turn **right**.
19.0 Turn **left** on **Logie Trail Road**.
21.6 Return to the starting point, Logie Trail Road and Highway 30.

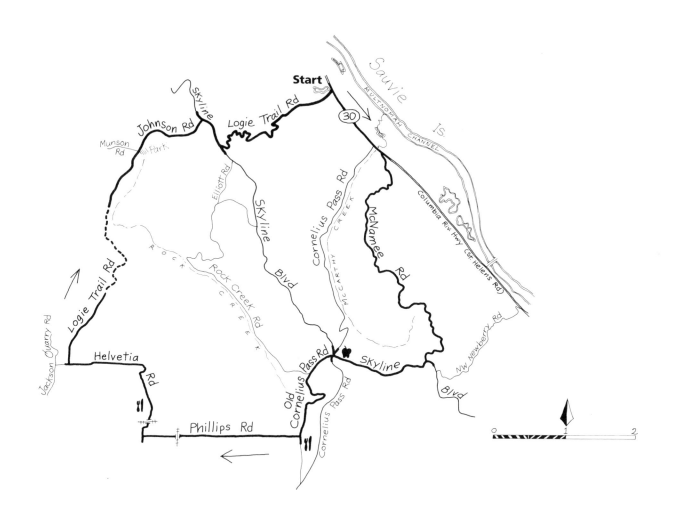

21 Lacamas Lake

**41 miles
from northeast Portland
challenging**

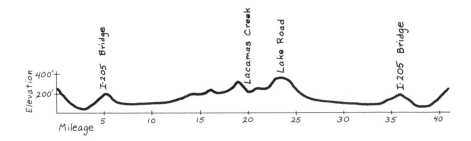

The Lacamas Lake Ride is a popular one among cyclists because there isn't much traffic, there are long continuous stretches, and several miles are along a separated bike path. Then there are the usual benefits of a good day ride: scenic views, colorful landscapes, and great exercise.

Lacamas Lake (also written "Lackamas" and "La Camas") was created when a dam was placed in Lacamas Creek. The loop goes around the lake, although the lake isn't in view much of the time. You ride along the east shore, then through some back country and hills, and finally to a spectacular stretch from the other side.

0.0 Begin at **Glenhaven Park**, N.E. 80th and Siskiyou Street in Portland. Ride north on 80th Avenue.
0.8 Stop sign at **Prescott Street**, turn **right**.
1.5 Turn **right** on the **bike path**, just after the freeway overpass.
1.6 Turn a sharp **right**, following the signs to Columbia Boulevard.
2.7 Follow the bike path signs across Columbia Boulevard and on toward Washington.
3.2 Turn **left** toward Washington Points, taking the Glen Jackson Bridge over the Columbia River.
5.1 Enter Washington State.
5.8 The bike path ends, turn **right** on **23rd Street**.
6.1 T-intersection at **Ellsworth Avenue**, turn **left**.
6.2 Stop sign at **Evergreen Highway**, turn **left**.
9.2 164th Avenue comes in on the left, continue straight.
13.1 Stop sign at **Highway 14**, turn **right**.
13.2 Turn **left** on **Logan Street**.
13.5 Turn **right** on **7th Street**.
13.6 Turn **left** on **Greeley Street**.
13.7 T-intersection at **10th Avenue**, turn **right**.
13.8 T-intersection at **Drake Street**, turn **left**.
14.0 Stop sign at **12th Avenue**, turn **right**.
14.1 Stop sign at **Division Street**, turn **left**.

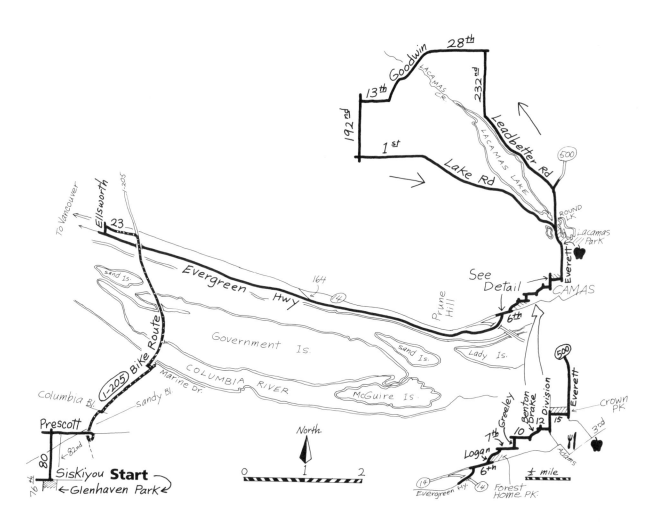

28th

Goodwin

13th

192nd

LACAMAS CR.

232nd

1st

Lake Rd

Leadbetter Rd

LACAMAS LAKE

500

ROUND LK.

Lacamas Park

Ellsworth

23

I-205

To Vancouver

Evergreen Hwy

164

14

sand Is.

Bike Route

See Detail

Everett

CAMAS

Prune Hill

6th

I-205 Bike Route

Government Is.

sand Is.

Lady Is.

500

Everett

Columbia Bl.

Marine Dr.

sandy Bl.

COLUMBIA RIVER

McGuire Is.

Crown PK.

3rd

Benton

Drake

Division

Greeley

Prescott

82nd

North

7th

Logan

10

15

Adams

80

Siskiyou **Start**

76th

←Glenhaven Park←

0   1   2

½ mile

14

14

Evergreen Hy.

6th

Forest Home PK.

14.3 Turn **right** at **15th Avenue**.
14.5 Stop sign at **Everett Street**, turn **left**.
15.5 Lacamas Park is on the right.
16.0 Turn **left** at **Leadbetter Road**, which becomes 232nd Avenue.
18.8 T-intersection at **28th Street**, turn **left**. 28th Street becomes Goodwin Road, then 13th Street.
20.1 Cross Lacamas Creek.
21.2 T-intersection at **192nd Avenue**, turn **left**.
21.9 Stop sign at **1st Avenue**, turn **left**. This becomes Lake Road.
25.7 T-intersection at **Everett Street**, turn **right**.
26.5 Turn **right** at **15th Avenue**.
26.7 Stop sign at **Division Street**, turn **left**.
26.8 Turn **right** at **12th Avenue**.
26.9 Stop sign at **Benton Street**, turn **left**. This becomes Drake Street.
27.1 Stop sign at **10th Avenue**, turn **right**.
27.3 Turn **left** on **Greeley Street**.
27.4 T-intersection at **7th Avenue**, turn **right**.
27.5 Turn **left** on **Logan Street**.
27.8 Stop sign at **Highway 14**, turn **right**.
27.9 Turn **left** on **6th Avenue**. This becomes **Evergreen Highway**.
31.8 164th Avenue comes in, turn **left** to stay on Evergreen Highway.
34.8 Turn **right** on **Ellsworth Avenue**.
34.9 Turn **right** on **23rd Street**.
35.2 Turn **left** onto the **bike path**.
37.5 Enter Portland.
37.9 Turn **right** on the bike path following the signs to Columbia Boulevard.
39.0 After crossing Columbia Boulevard as marked with the bike signs, turn left from Columbia onto the bike path.
39.4 Turn **left** from the bike path toward **Prescott Street**.
39.5 Turn **left** on **Prescott Street**.
40.2 Turn **left** on **80th Avenue**.
41.0 Return to **Glenhaven Park**.

22 Mt. Scott

18 miles
from southeast Portland
challenging

Mt. Scott gives Portland cyclists a great hill-climbing challenge. The top is 1087 feet above sea level, and you climb almost 900 feet of it in three miles. Along with the great climb, you of course get great views—Mt. Hood, Mt. Adams, Mt. Rainier (on a clear day), and Mt. St. Helens. The descent is also great, but it's always so short we quickly forget it.

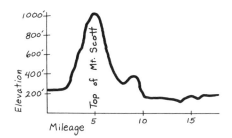

0.0 Begin at **Mt. Scott Park**, S.E. 72nd and Harold Street in Portland. Ride south on 72nd Avenue.

1.0 Four-way stop sign at **Flavel Street**, turn **left**. This becomes Mt. Scott Boulevard.

4.1 Turn **right** on **Idleman Road**, just before Mt. Scott Boulevard goes downhill.

4.4 Turn **right** on **Tyler Road**, just before Idleman goes downhill.

4.6 Turn **right** on **Eastview Drive**, just as Tyler goes downhill. There are good views here.

4.9 The road curves left to become Ridgeway Drive.

5.1 Stop at the corner before the road heads downhill. You have reached the summit, congratulations! Enjoy the view. Then turn around and head back.

5.6 T-intersection at **Tyler Street**, turn **left**.

5.9 T-intersection at **Idleman Road**, turn **left**.

6.2 Stop sign at **Mt. Scott Boulevard**, turn **right**. This becomes King Road.

6.8 Turn **right** on **129th Avenue**. This becomes 122nd Avenue.

8.5 Turn **right** on **Mather Road**.

10.3 Turn **left** on **Industrial Way**.

10.6 Turn **left** on **Clackamas Road**.

10.6 Turn **right** on **98th Avenue**.

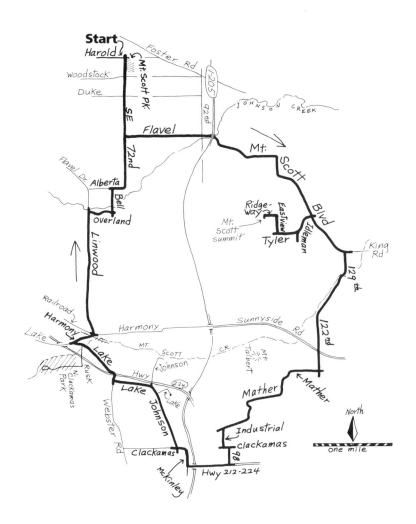

10.8 Stop sign at **Highway 212/224**, turn **right**. This highway has a lot of traffic, so you may want to take advantage of the sidewalk.

11.4 T-intersection at **McKinley Avenue**, turn **right** toward Clackamas Road.

11.7 Turn **right** on **Johnson Road**.

12.6 Turn **left** to **Lake Road**.

13.1 Traffic light at **Webster Road**, turn **right**. This becomes Lake Road.

13.9 Traffic light at **Harmony Road**, turn **right**.

14.2 Light at Harmony/Railroad Avenue, go **straight** onto **Linwood Avenue**.

15.8 Turn **right** to **Overland Street** just before the creek bridge.

16.1 Stop sign at **Bell Avenue**, turn **left**.

16.4 T-intersection at **Alberta Avenue**, turn **right**. This curves left to become 72nd Avenue.

18.3 Return to **Mt. Scott Park** at Harold Street.

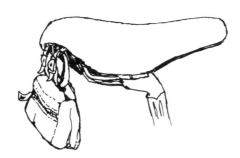

Climbing Hills

Good cycling techniques can make a hill more enjoyable, or at least make it possible. Shift to an easy pedaling gear well before the hill. Establish a rhythm you can maintain through the climb—this uses less energy than pedaling hard and then coasting. Standing up is sometimes good for variety or for the last push over the top, but it's hard to maintain. When you're sitting on the saddle, if you put your hands on the top of the handlebars or over the brake lever hoods you expand your lungs for easier breathing.

Beware of mental traps. Avoid watching your feet, thinking about your knees, and repeating silly jingles. Instead, make your mind think to identify the plants, remember the Gettysburg Address, or plan your next ride. Stopping to rest is not against the rules and may be beneficial physically and mentally. Drink water, look at the view, turn around to see how far you've come.

Aah the descent! Alas, it's so short. The most stable position is sitting back and low, hands on the drops, and with the inside pedal up when you go through a corner. Keep good control on the brakes, slow down before the turns, and remember that the front brake gives you twice the stopping power as your rear brake.

23 Rocky Butte and Mt. Tabor

14 miles
from northeast Portland
challenging

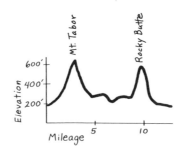

Each one of these hills is a commendable bike ride, but we've put them together to make sure you get your aerobic exercise. Rocky Butte and Mt. Tabor are extinct volcanoes, formed several million years ago. As city parks today, these two hills are quite different, each with its special appeal— Rocky Butte offers rock climbers a great practice area, and Mt. Tabor shows an exposed volcanic cinder cone.

0.0 Start at **Normandale Park**, N.E. 57th and Halsey Street in Portland. Ride south on 57th Street, which turns into Hassalo Street.
0.3 T-intersection at **55th Street**, turn **left**. This turns into Irving Street.
0.5 Stop sign at **53rd Avenue**, turn **left**.
1.4 T-intersection at **Taylor Street**, turn **left**.
1.5 T-intersection at **55th Avenue**, turn **right**.
1.6 Turn **left** on **Salmon Street**. Keep on Salmon Street up into Mt. Tabor Park.
2.1 Follow the main park road as it makes a hairpin left turn.
2.5 Follow the main park road right and up past the playground equipment.
2.7 Still stay on the main road, straight through this intersection.
3.0 Top of Mt. Tabor; curve **right** around the top, and head downhill.
3.6 At the first intersection from the top, turn **right**.
4.2 Make a hairpin **left** turn, by the park sign. This becomes Harrison Street.
4.6 T-intersection at **76th Avenue**, turn **left**.
5.3 T-intersection at **Stark Street**, turn **left**.
5.4 Turn **right** on **74th Avenue**.
6.4 Traffic signal at Halsey Street, **jog left** to stay on **74th Avenue**.
6.7 T-intersection at **Tillamook Street**, turn **left**.
6.8 Turn **right** on **72nd Drive**.
7.2 T-intersection at **Sacramento Street**, turn **right**.
7.3 Turn **left** on **72nd Avenue**.

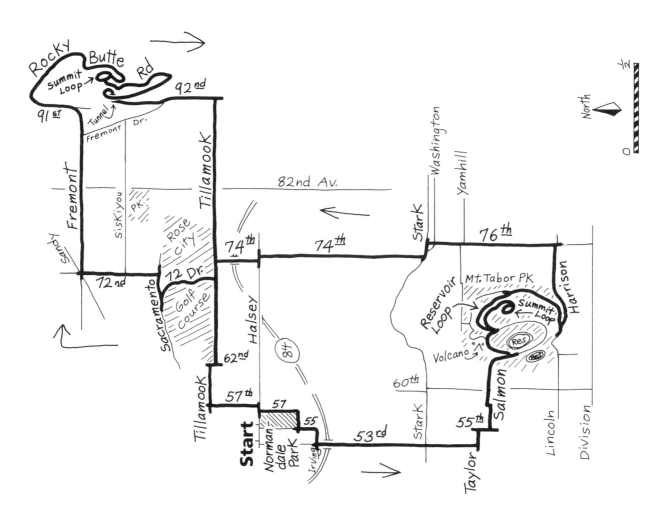

7.7 Traffic light at Fremont Street and Sandy Boulevard, turn **right** on **Fremont**.

8.7 Fremont curves left and becomes 91st Street.

9.8 The top of Rocky Butte. Walk up to the top of the rock formation for a spectacular panoramic view. Then follow the road around to the right, as the arrow indicates.

10.0 Take the first road to the right to descend (this is not the same road you came up). *Be cautious through the hairpin turn through the tunnel.

11.4 Stop sign at **92nd Avenue**, continue **straight**.

11.6 Turn **right** on **Tillamook Street**.

13.1 T-intersection at 62nd Avenue, **jog right** to stay on **Tillamook Street**.

13.4 Stop sign at **57th Avenue**, turn **left**.

13.7 Traffic light at **Halsey Street**, **jog right** to return to Normandale Park.

24 Salmon Creek

26 miles
from Vancouver, Washington
challenging

Many Portland cyclists are unaware of the wonderful miles of good riding just north of the Columbia River. Salmon Creek is just one of the pastoral parts of this ride through orchards, dairy farms, woodlands, and a unique bird refuge. There are several short steep inclines on this loop along quiet roads of Clark County.

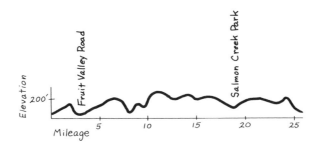

0.0 **Esther Short Park**, on 8th and Columbia Street in Vancouver, Washington, is the starting point. Start westward on 8th Street.

0.1 Turn **right** on **Franklin Street**.

0.4 Stop sign at **13th Street**, turn **left**.

0.6 Turn **right** on **Kauffman Avenue**.

1.9 Stop sign at **39th Street**, turn **left**.

2.5 T-intersection at **Fruit Valley Road**, turn **right**. This becomes Lakeshore Avenue, then 31st Avenue.

6.7 The main road curves **left** and becomes **119th Street**, then curves **right** and becomes **36th Avenue**. This same road is later called Seward Road, then 41st Avenue.

10.3 Turn **right** on **179th Avenue** toward Vancouver.

14.8 Stop sign at **50th Avenue**, turn **right**.

16.3 Stop sign at **Salmon Creek Street**, turn **right**.

19.1 Stop sign at **Highway 99**, turn **left**, then **right** on **Klineline Road**.

19.3 Stop sign at **117th Street**, turn **right**.

19.5 Salmon Creek Park on the right, with restrooms, picnicking, and swimming in season. The road becomes Hazel Dell Avenue.

23.6 Turn **right** on the "**Dead End**" street just before Main Street. Follow the bike route signs.

23.7 Cross Highway 99 with the bike route and follow the path downhill into Leverich Park.

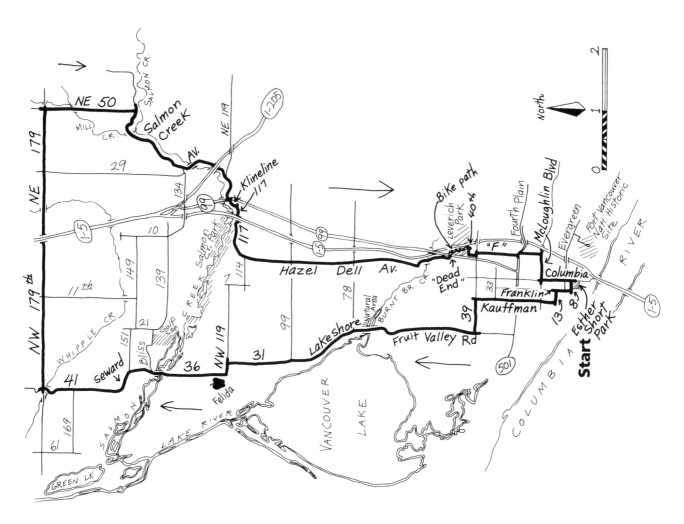

NE 50

NE 179

NE 179th

Salmon Creek

Salmon Cr.

Mill Cr.

29

134

Kline line 117

NE 119

I-205

99

I-5

10

149

139

Salmon Cr. Park

11th

Whipple Cr.

151

21

Bliss

Seward

41

36

NW 119

NW 179th

Felida

Green Lk.

Lake River

Salmon River

114

7

117

31

Lakeshore

99

78

Burnt Br. Cr.

I-5 99

Natural Area

Fruit Valley Rd

501

Vancouver Lake

Columbia River

Bike path

Leverich Park

40th

"Dead End"

"F"

39

Kauffman

Franklin

33

13

Fourth Plain

McLoughlin Blvd

Evergreen

Columbia

8

Fort Vancouver Nat. Historic Site

I-5

Esther Short Park

Start

North

0 1 2

24.1 Turn **right** on **40th Street**, with the bike route.

24.3 Turn **left** on **F Street**.

24.4 **Jog left** at 39th Street to stay on **F Street**.

25.1 **Jog left** at Fourth Plain Boulevard to stay on **F Street**.

25.4 Stop sign at **McLoughlin Boulevard**, turn **right**.

25.8 Traffic light at **Columbia Street**, turn **left**.

26.4 Return to **Esther Short Park**, at 8th Street.

25 Skyline

39 miles
from northwest Portland
challenging

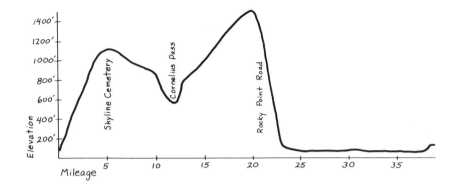

Skyline Boulevard, one of the older roads in the area, is included in the 1896 "Cyclists' Road Map of Portland." Perhaps originally constructed as a logging road, Skyline has always been noted for its splendid views of the mountains and valleys. And still today, the best way to observe these views is from your bicycle seat.

Skyline Boulevard leads you along the crest of the Tualatin Mountains, so there are climbs. Many cyclists have ridden sections of Skyline, but this route shows off the whole length.

0.0 Start at **Wallace Park**, N.W. 25th and Raleigh Street in Portland. Ride south on 25th Avenue.

0.3 Four-way stop at **Lovejoy Street**, turn **right**. The road soon curves right and becomes **Cornell Road**.

1.1 First of two tunnels on Cornell Road.

1.4 Second tunnel.

3.4 Summit along Cornell Road, turn **right** on **Skyline Boulevard**.

12.4 Intersection with Cornelius Pass Road. Keep on Skyline by heading right slightly, crossing the street and pedaling up the hill.

13.4 Views of Mt. Rainier, Mt. St. Helens, and Mt. Adams.

20.5 Turn **right** on **Rocky Point Road**, as Skyline curves left and becomes Dixie Mountain Road.

23.7 Stop sign at **Highway 30** (St. Helens Road), turn **right**.

28.6 Burlington community, with a store and a cafe.

29.3 Views of Mt. Hood, Mt. Adams, Mt. St. Helens, and Mt. Rainier.

32.7 Linnton community, store and cafe.

36.8 Traffic signal at Kittridge Avenue, turn **right** to stay on **St. Helens Road** (Highway 30).

38.6 Traffic signal at **29th Avenue**, turn **right**.

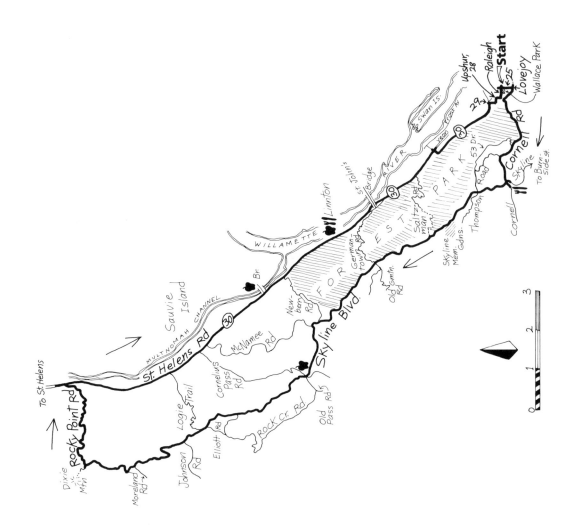

38.7 The road curves left and becomes **Upshur Street**.
38.8 Upshur curves right and becomes **28th Avenue**.
39.0 Turn **left** on **Raleigh Street**.
39.3 Return to **Wallace Park** at 25th Avenue and Raleigh Street.

26 West Union

31 miles
from northwest Portland
challenging

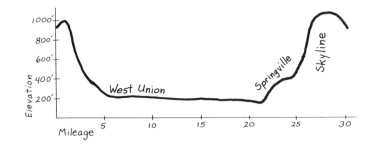

There's wonderful biking country just to the west of Portland, at least until the developers get to it. The roads on this loop have long been popular with cyclists, whether they're training for a race or enjoying a good scenic ride.

There are good hills on Thompson, Springville and Skyline Boulevard, but the roads west of 185th Avenue are pretty level. As you ride through the rural land, you'll see barns, wheatfields, horses, hawks (we saw a coyote once), and probably other cyclists.

0.0 Start at the intersection of **N.W. Skyline Boulevard** and **Cornell Road**. Head north on Skyline toward Skyline Memorial Gardens.
0.9 Four-way stop sign at **Thompson Road**, turn **left**, and follow Thompson as it curves around.
4.0 Stop sign at Saltzman Road, cross Saltzman and continue on **Thompson**.
5.1 After passing Hartung Farms, **West Union Road** comes in on the **right**, **turn** onto it.
10.7 West Union Road crosses Helvetia Road.
13.6 Turn **left** at **Jackson Road**.
15.4 Turn **left** on **Meek Road**.
17.9 Stop sign at **Shute Road**, turn **left**. Shute Road is called Helvetia Road after it crosses Highway 26.
18.9 Turn **right** at **West Union Road**.
22.0 Four-way intersection at **185th Avenue**, turn **left**.
22.3 Stop sign at **Springville Road**, turn **right**. After three miles of mild hills, you begin a 1½-mile continuous uphill stretch.
26.8 T-intersection at **Skyline Boulevard**, turn **right**.
29.5 Four-way stop at Thompson Road, continue straight on Skyline.
30.5 Cornell Road intersects with Skyline Boulevard, end of loop.

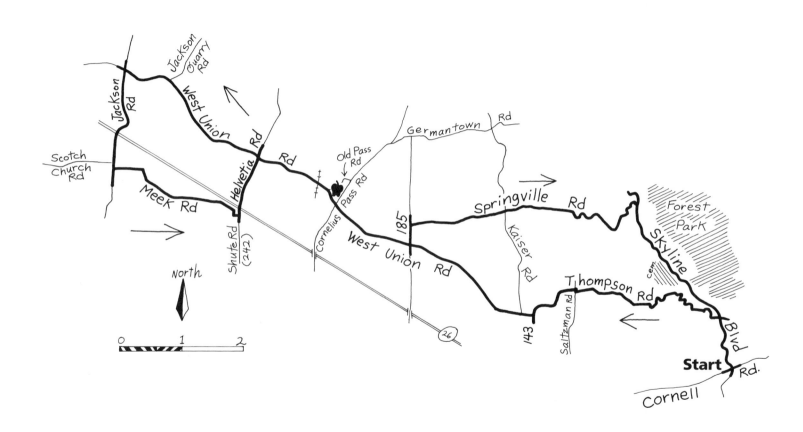

North

0   1   2

Start

27 Battle Ground Lake

Campground for overnight
Day 1: 28 miles
Day 2: 41 miles
from northeast Portland
challenging

Here's a trip into the foothills of the Cascades that, in just one day on your bike, brings you closer to the wilderness. The backroads of rural Clark County have little traffic, exotic wildlife, and untamed hills. You may be in for some surprises.

Battle Ground Lake was formed the same way Crater Lake was formed: a large volcanic cone collapsed on itself. It's a beautiful setting for swimming, fishing, relaxing, or exploring. An overnight stay in the campground (Washington State Park system) will give you time to scout around.

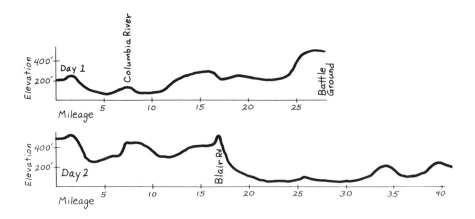

Day 1

0.0 Start at **Normandale Park**, N.E. 57th and Halsey Street in Portland. Jog right across Halsey at the signal and go north on 57th Avenue.
0.3 Turn **right** on **Tillamook Street**.
0.5 T-intersection at **62nd Avenue**. Jog **right**, then **left** on **Tillamook**.
1.0 Turn left on **72nd Drive** and ride through the Rose City Golf Course.
1.4 T-intersection at **Sacramento Street**, turn **right**.
1.5 Turn **left** on **72nd Avenue**.
2.4 Flashing light at **Prescott Street**, turn **right**.
3.5 Turn **right** on the **bike path**, just after the viaduct over I-205.
3.6 Turn **right** at the fork, following the signs to Columbia Boulevard, and farther.
5.2 Turn **left** toward Washington Points, and cross over the Columbia River.
7.9 Bike path ends, turn **right** onto **23rd Street**.
8.2 T-intersection at **Ellsworth Road**, turn **left**.
8.3 Stop sign at **Evergreen Highway**, turn **left**.
11.3 Veer **left** at the fork toward the stop sign. Turn **left** toward State Highway 14 (164th Avenue). This becomes 162nd Avenue.

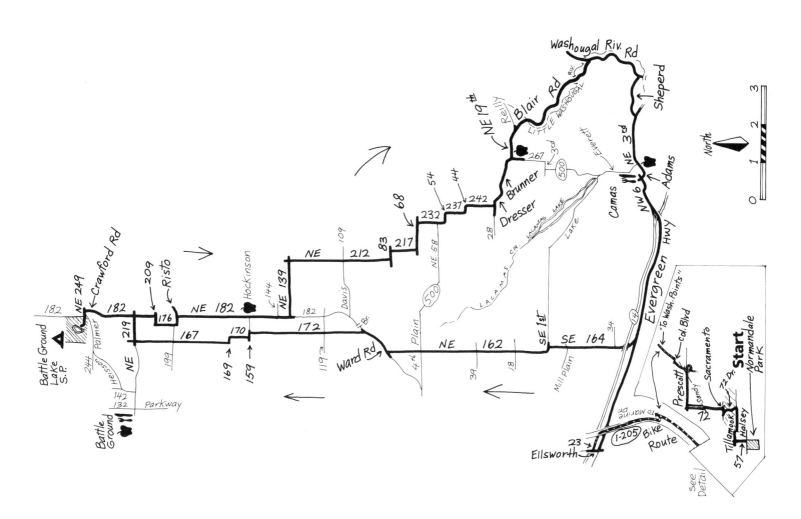

17.9 T-intersection at **Ward Road**, turn **right**.

18.6 Turn **left** on **172nd Avenue**, just before the creek bridge.

21.7 T-intersection at **159th Street**, turn **left**.

21.8 Turn **right** on **170th Avenue**. This becomes 169th Street, then 167th Avenue.

25.0 Stop sign at **219th Street**, turn **right**.

25.7 Stop sign at **182nd Avenue**, turn **left** toward Battle Ground Lake. This becomes Crawford Road.

27.3 Cross 182nd/Palmer Road into Battle Ground Park.

27.5 Battle Ground Park. Enjoy the lake, camping, trails, wildlife.

Day 2

0.0 Leave Battle Ground Park, cross 182nd/Palmer and continue on Crawford Road.

0.3 Curve right with the road, staying on Crawford. This turns into 182nd Avenue, 209th Street, then 176th Avenue.

3.1 T-intersection at **Risto Road**, turn **left**.

3.4 Curve **right** with the main road, which becomes **182nd Avenue**.

6.3 Turn **left** on **139th Street**, toward Clark Rifles, and go up the steep hill.

7.8 Stop sign at **212th Avenue**, turn **right**.

10.6 T-intersection at **83rd Street**, turn **left**.

10.8 Turn **right** on **217th Avenue**.

11.6 T-intersection at **68th Street**, turn **left**.

12.3 Turn **right** with the road, to **232nd Avenue**.

12.8 Stop sign at 58th Street, continue **straight** on **232nd Avenue**. This curves to become 54th Street, then 237th Avenue, then 44th Street, then 242nd Avenue (why do they do this to us?).

14.7 T-intersection at **Dresser Road**, also called **Highway 500**. Turn **left**. This changes its name to Brunner Road.

16.1 Turn **left** on **19th Street**, just after Brunner turns right.

16.7 Turn **right** on **Blair Road** and sail downhill along the Little Washougal River.

Preventive Maintenance
Part I The Bicycle

- Keep tires inflated to the recommended pressure.
- Lubricate the chain monthly.
- Fix squeaks, knocks, thunks when they first appear.
- Have your bicycle overhauled once a year.

20.1 T-intersection at **Washougal River Road**, turn **right**.
21.9 Turn **right** on **Sheperd Road**, before the bridge.
23.0 T-intersection at **3rd Avenue**, turn **right**.
24.6 Turn **right** on **Adams Street**, as the light indicates.
24.8 Turn **left** on **6th Avenue**/Highway 14.
25.7 Turn **left** on **6th Avenue**/Evergreen Highway, marked by the sign to Washougal (although you don't go to Washougal).
29.7 Take the **left fork** where 164th comes in, to stay on **Evergreen Highway.**
32.7 Turn **right** on **Ellsworth Road**.
32.8 Turn **right** on **23rd Street**.
33.0 Turn **left** onto the bike path.
35.8 T-intersection in the bike path, turn **right** toward Columbia Boulevard. Follow the bike route signs through the Columbia Boulevard intersection.
37.4 Turn **left** from the bike path toward Prescott Street.
37.4 Turn **left** on **Prescott Street**.
38.6 Stop sign at **72nd Avenue**, turn **left**.
39.1 Traffic signal at Sandy Boulevard, **jog left** to stay on **72nd Avenue**.
39.5 T-intersection at **Sacramento Street**, turn **right**.
39.6 Turn **left** on **72nd Drive**.
40.0 Stop sign at **Tillamook Street**, turn **right**.
40.5 Stop sign at 62nd Avenue, **jog right** to continue on **Tillamook**.
40.8 Stop sign at **57th Avenue**, turn **left**.
41.1 Traffic signal at **Halsey Street**, **jog right** to return to the starting point, **Normandale Park**.

28 Columbia River Gorge

**Campground for overnight
35 miles each day
from southeast Portland
challenging**

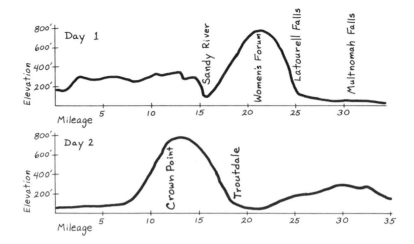

Lots of cyclists ride up the gorge for a challenging day ride, but we suggest you take your sleeping bag and spend the night, so you can take the time to enjoy all the waterfalls, side gorges, views, and flowers. The hill to Crown Point is not easy, especially on the return trip your second day. But this area is so wonderful you enjoy every inch of the hill. You certainly have time to.

Ainsworth State Park is open May through October. The park is closed in the winter, and the road may also be closed—it sometimes is filled with snow or rock slides.

Day 1

0.0 Laurelhurst Park is the take-off point, at S.E. 37th and Oak Street in Portland. Ride south on 37th Avenue.

0.8 Stop sign at **Lincoln Street**, turn **left**.

2.2 Where Lincoln Street turns right, turn **left** into **Mt. Tabor Park**.

2.5 Turn **right** at the fork, downhill.

2.7 Stop sign at **72nd Avenue**, turn **left**, for one block.

2.8 Turn **right** on **Stephens Street**.

3.0 Stop sign at 76th Avenue, jog **right**, then **left** to stay on **Stephens Street**.

3.2 T-intersection at **80th Avenue**, turn **left**, for one block.

3.2 Turn **right** on **Mill Street**.

3.8 Stop sign at **92nd Avenue**, turn **left**.

3.8 Turn **right** on **Market Street**.

5.8 T-intersection at **130th Avenue**, turn **right**.

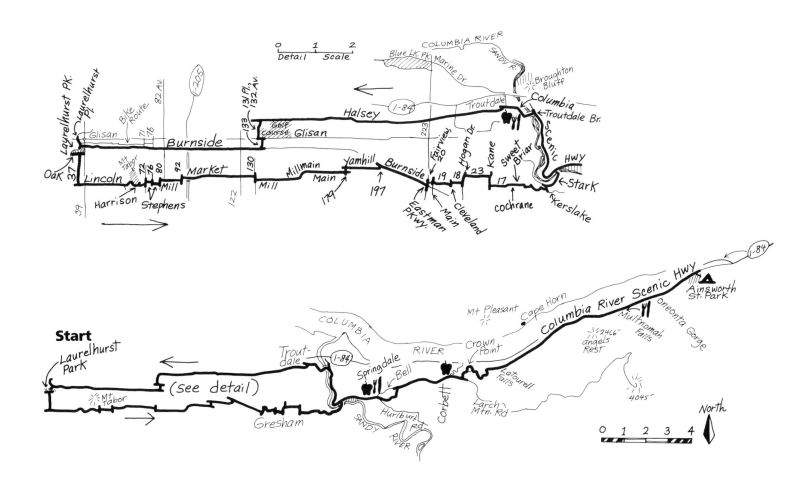

Detail scale

0   1   2
Detail   scale

COLUMBIA RIVER

Blue Lk. Pk. Marine Dr.   SANDY R.

Broughton Bluff

Laurelhurst Pk.
Laurelhurst Pl.

Bike Route

82 Av.

I-205

131 Pl.,
132 Av.

133

I-84

Troutdale

Columbia

Troutdale Br.

Glisan   71
76

Burnside   Golf course

Glisan

Halsey

223

Scenic Hwy

Oak   37

Lincoln   Mt. Tabor   72
76
80   92

Market   130

Millmain   Yamhill

Burnside   Fairview
20   Hogan Dr.   Kane

Sweet Briar

39   Harrison
Stephens   Mill   Mill   Main   179   191   Eastman Pkwy.   19   18   23   17   cochrane   Kerslake   Stark

122

Cleveland   Main

Start
Laurelhurst Park

Mt. Tabor

(see detail)

Gresham

Troutdale   I-84

Springdale   Bell

COLUMBIA   RIVER

Hurlburt Rd.

SANDY RIVER

Corbett

Larch Mtn. Rd

Mt Pleasant   Cape Horn

Crown Point

Columbia River Scenic Hwy

Latourell Falls

2466
angels Rest

Multnomah Falls

Oneonta Gorge

Ainsworth St. Park

I-84

4045

0 1 2 3 4   North

5.9 Turn **left** on **Mill Street**, following the bike route. This becomes **Millmain Drive**, then **Main Street**.

8.5 Turn **left** on **179th Avenue**, with the bike route.

8.6 Turn **right** on **Yamhill Street**. Yamhill curves left and becomes **197th Avenue**.

9.6 Traffic light at **Burnside Street**, turn **right**.

10.9 Traffic light at **Eastman Parkway**, turn **left**.

11.0 Turn **right** on **Fairview Drive**, then **left** on **20th Street**.

11.1 T-intersection at **Main Avenue**, jog **right**, then **left** on **19th Street**.

11.7 Stop sign at Cleveland Avenue; jog **left** to get on **18th Street**.

12.0 T-intersection at **Hogan Drive**, turn **left**.

12.2 Turn **right** on **23rd Street**.

12.9 T-intersection at **Kane Drive**, turn **right**.

13.1 Turn **left** on **17th Street**. This becomes **Cochrane**, then **Sweet Briar Road**.

14.6 Curve **left** to stay on **Sweet Briar Road**.

14.9 Turn **left** on **Kerslake Road**, during a nice downhill run.

15.0 T-intersection at **Stark Street**, turn **right**.

15.6 After crossing the bridge, you come to a T-intersection at the **Scenic Highway**, turn **right**.

16.0 Dabney State Park is on the right.

17.1 Springdale, grocery store.

17.4 Curve **right** to stay on the Scenic Highway.

17.5 Curve **left** to stay on the Scenic Highway.

19.7 Corbett.

20.4 Take the **left** fork to stay on the Scenic Highway.

21.5 Women's Forum State Park.

21.9 Curve **left** to stay on the Scenic Highway.

22.7 Vista House on Crown Point. Open May 1 through October 15. This is a beautiful building with a wonderful history of the road you're traveling.

25.1 Latourell Falls.

26.3 Shepperds Dell.

Preventive Maintenance
Part II The Rider

• Drink before you're thirsty.
• Eat before you're hungry.
• Shift before the hill.

27.2 Bridal Veil.

30.5 Wahkeena Falls.

31.0 Multnomah Falls. Restaurant and snack bar, not to mention gorgeous waterfall.

33.3 Oneonta Gorge.

33.6 Horsetail Falls.

34.1 Pass Ainsworth Park Picnic Area.

34.6 Turn **right** to enter **Ainsworth Campground**.

Day 2

0.0 Leave Ainsworth Park, heading back toward Portland on the Scenic Highway.

12.0 Vista House on Crown Point.

17.5 Springdale.

18.6 Dabney State Park is on the left. Continue on the Scenic Highway toward Troutdale.

21.4 Turn **left** with the road, crossing the Troutdale bridge over the Sandy River. This becomes **Columbia Boulevard**.

22.1 Troutdale. Restaurant, groceries.

22.4 Curve **left** toward Wood Village, on **Halsey Street**.

23.7 Wood Village. Groceries.

29.1 Traffic light at **131st Place/**132nd Avenue, turn **left**.

29.6 Stop sign at **Glisan Street**, turn **left**.

29.7 Turn **right** on **133rd Avenue**.

29.9 T-intersection at **Burnside Street**, turn **right**. The bike route from 71st Avenue will take you safely to Laurelhurst.

34.9 Turn **left** on **Laurelhurst Place after 39th Avenue**.

35.0 **Laurelhurst Park** at Ankeny Street. To get to Oak Street where you began, walk your bike straight through the park on the paved path.

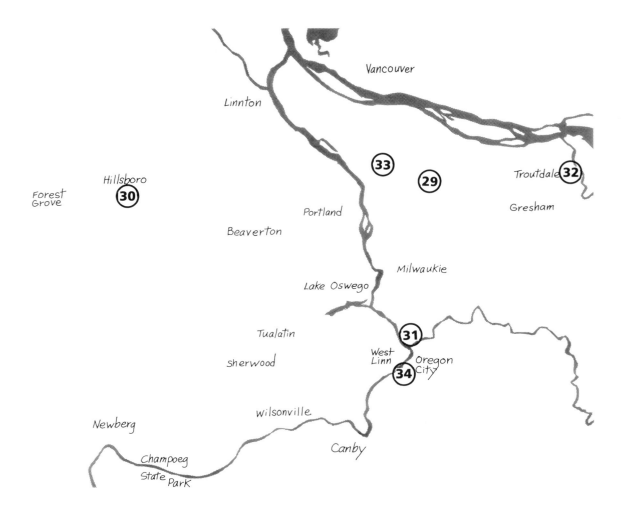

Forest
Grove

Hillsboro
(30)

Linnton

Vancouver

(33)

(29)

Troutdale (32)

Gresham

Portland

Beaverton

Milwaukie

Lake Oswego

Tualatin

Sherwood

West
Linn (31)
Oregon
City
(34)

Wilsonville

Newberg

Champoeg
State Park

Canby

Most Difficult Rides

29 Bridge of the Gods

86 miles
from northeast Portland
most difficult

This ride up the Columbia Gorge is a classic for dedicated distance riders. The scenery is constantly spectacular, the climbs and descents are exhilarating, and the food is available at just the right places.

The weather in the gorge is important to consider when doing this ride. The winds blow strong up or down the gorge, which means you may have to pedal against a 25-mile-per-hour headwind for half the trip. Summer winds are more likely west to east; in the fall and winter east winds are more common. Winds blow stronger on higher exposed places—like the bridge itself.

Rainfall is a lot higher at Cascade Locks than in Portland, and snow and ice on the Scenic Highway can close the road in the winter. But on a sunny fall day, this is one of the best long distance rides from Portland.

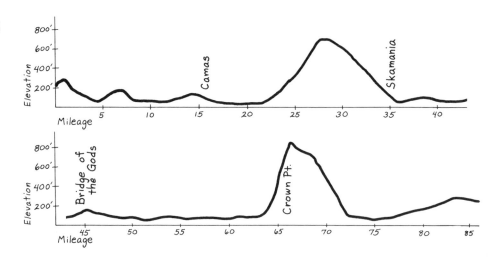

0.0 **Montavilla Park**, N.E. 82nd and Glisan Street, is the beginning point. Travel east on Glisan.

0.7 Stop on the sidewalk at the bike route just after the viaduct over I-205. Press the button to be able to cross Glisan and ride north on the bike path, following the signs.

4.5 Turn **left** on the bike path following the signs to Washington Points.

7.2 Bike path ends, turn **right** (23rd Street, unmarked).

7.5 T-intersection at **Ellsworth Avenue**, turn **left**.

7.6 Stop sign at **Evergreen Highway**, turn **left**.

14.7 Stop sign at **6th Avenue**, turn **right** toward Camas.

15.7 Stop sign at **Adams Street**, turn **right** following the signs for Highway 14 and Highway 500. There are stores and restaurants around here.

15.8 Flashing yellow light at **3rd Avenue**, turn **left**.

16.0 Traffic light at **Dallas Street**, turn **right** toward Highway 14.

17.0 Stop sign at **Highway 14**, turn **left**.

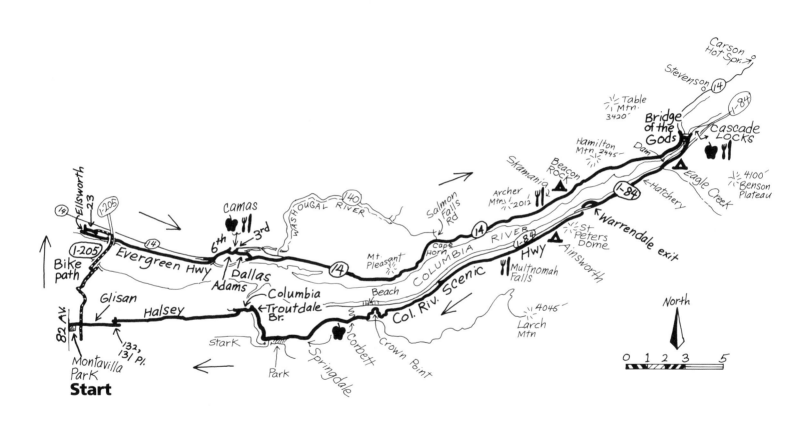

Carson
Hot Spr.

Stevenson
14

Table
Mtn.
3420

Bridge
of the
Gods

Cascade
LOCKS

I-84

Hamilton
Mtn. 2445

Beacon
Rock

Skamania

Dam

4100
Benson
Plateau

Eagle Creek

←Hatchery

Archer
Mtn. -2012

I-84

St
Peters
Dome

Warrendale exit

Salmon
Falls
Rd

COLUMBIA RIVER

14

Ellsworth
-23

14   I-205

Camas

6th   3rd

40

WASHOUGAL RIVER

Cape
Horn

Mt.
Pleasant

Hwy

Ainsworth

Multnomah
Falls

I-205

Evergreen Hwy

14

Dallas
Adams

14

Beach

Col. Riv. Scenic

Bike
path

82 Av.

Glisan   Halsey

Columbia
←Troutdale
Br.

Stark

Corbett

Crown Point

4045
Larch
Mtn

North

Montavilla
Park
Start

132,
131 Pl.

Park

Springdale

0 1 2 3   5

27.6 Good view, one of many along here.

35.5 Skamania, with a grocery store and a restaurant.

37.3 Beacon Rock State Park on the right.

44.2 Turn **right** to the **Bridge of the Gods**. This is a toll bridge, cyclists pay 25¢ (even though you've been pedaling for hours).

44.9 Cascade Locks. Restaurants and stores are here. Turn **left** toward Portland on **Highway 30** Westbound, which becomes the I-84 freeway, where you ride on the shoulder, carefully.

50.6 Take the **Warrendale Exit**, #37.

51.1 Turn **left**, toward Dodson and Portland. Then at the T-intersection turn **right**. This is the Columbia Gorge Scenic Highway.

52.9 T-intersection, turn **left** toward Multnomah Falls and Portland.

53.2 T-intersection, turn **left** to the **Scenic Highway** (not right to Portland via I-84).

53.6 Ainsworth State Park.

54.5 Horsetail Falls.

54.9 Oneonta Gorge.

57.1 Multnomah Falls, with a restaurant and snack bar.

57.7 Wahkeena Falls, picnic area.

60.2 Take the **left fork**, to stay on the Scenic Highway, toward Crown Point.

61.1 Bridal Veil State Park.

61.9 Shepperds Dell.

63.1 Latourell Falls.

65.6 Vista House at Crown Point State Park.

66.7 Women's Forum State Park.

68.5 Corbett. Grocery store.

71.2 Springdale. Store, restaurant.

72.3 Dabney State Park.

75.1 Turn **left** with the road, crossing the Troutdale Bridge over the Sandy River. This becomes Columbia Boulevard.

75.8 Town of Troutdale.

76.1 Curve **left** toward Wood Village on **Halsey Street**.

The Bridge of the Gods

There was once a great land bridge of peace connecting the lands of the Multnomah Indians and the Klickitat Indians. However, Chief Wyeast to the south (Mt. Hood) and Chief Pahto to the north (Mt. Adams) both fell in love with the beautiful Loowit (Mt. St. Helens) and their jealousy led to angry—and sometimes volcanic—fighting. The Great Spirit was dismayed by the fighting, and broke down the Bridge of the Gods.

Modern geologists note this narrow spot of the river and deduce that there had been a great landslide 700 years ago. So much land slid that it pushed the river course a mile away and dammed up the river for a while, creating a vast lake behind it. Through erosion the river channel has opened up.

Road engineers in 1926 took advantage of this narrow area of the Columbia River and built a bridge to connect the lands once again.

82.8 Traffic light at **131st Place/132nd Avenue**, turn **left**.
83.3 Stop sign at **Glisan Street**, turn **right**.
85.9 Return to **Montavilla Park**, 82nd and Glisan Street.

30 Chehalem Mountain

51 miles
from Hillsboro
most difficult

The climb to the summit of Chehalem Mountain is long and steady, allowing you to appreciate the patchwork pattern of farmlands on the hill and in the Tualatin Valley. In the spring, when the trees on the upper slopes are sporting their white blossoms, the effect is like climbing into a sky filled with popcorn. The downhill run into Newberg is delightfully swift and curving, and as you turn north again you see the impressive steep side of the mountains.

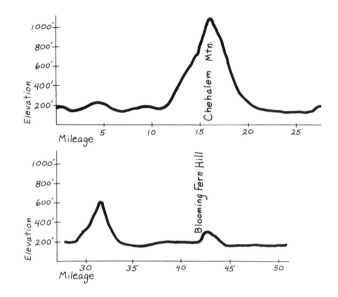

0.0 Start at **Shute Park**, 10th and Maple Street in Hillsboro. Ride east on Maple Street.
0.2 Stop sign at **13th Avenue**, turn **right**.
0.6 Cross Tualatin Valley Highway with the traffic signal onto **River Road**.
1.9 Traffic signal at **Rood Bridge Road**, turn **right**.
5.8 T-intersection at **Farmington Highway**, turn **left**.
6.6 Stop sign at **River Road**, turn **right**.
9.5 Stop sign at **Highway 210** (Scholls Ferry Road), turn **right**.
11.3 Scholls; go **straight**. The highway becomes **Highway 219**.
16.3 Summit of Chehalem Mountain. Follow Highway 219 down to Newberg (it becomes College Street in Newberg).
21.7 Traffic signal at **Hancock Street** (Highway 99W), one-way westbound. Turn **right**.

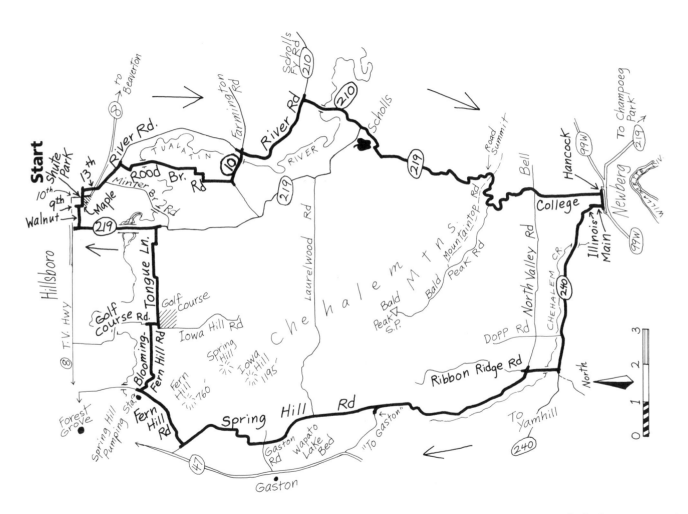

22.1 Traffic signal at **Highway 240**, turn **right**. This is called Main Street, then it curves left and is called Illinois Street in Newberg.

27.7 Four-way intersection, turn **right** onto **Ribbon Ridge Road**, following the sign "To Gaston."

28.5 Four-way intersection, go **left** on **North Valley Road**, "To Gaston."

33.4 At the Y-intersection marked with left turn arrows to Gaston, go **straight** on **Springhill Road**.

40.0 Y-intersection, turn **right** on **Fernhill Road**.

42.2 Turn **right** on **Blooming-Fern Hill Road**, across the road from the Spring Hill Pumping Plant. This is very steep for .2 miles, so shift before the hill!

44.5 T-intersection at **Golf Course Road**, turn **right**.

44.8 T-intersection at **Tongue Lane**, turn **left**.

47.8 T-intersection at **Highway 219**, turn **left**.

50.2 Turn **right** onto **Walnut Street**.

51.0 Turn **right** on **9th Avenue**, and return to **Shute Park** on Maple Street.

31 Clackamas River

43 miles
from Clackamette Park in Oregon City
most difficult

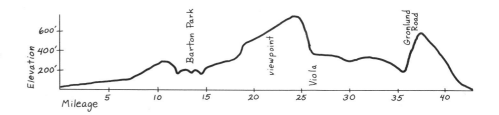

From its beginning in the Cascade crest near Olallie Lake, the Clackamas River has carved through a slice of beautiful Oregon country. Starting at the finishing end of the waters, called Clackamette Park, this ride shows you a river gorge, quiet rich parks, spectacular mountain views, a historic log cabin, various creek crossings, productive farmlands, and modern urban buildings.

0.0 Clackamette Park sits on the Willamette and Clackamas Rivers, just off Highway 99E in Oregon City. Turn **left** out of the park onto **Main Street**.
0.8 Turn **left** on **17th Street**.
0.9 Traffic light at **Washington Street**, turn **left**.
1.6 Traffic light at **Clackamas River Road**, turn **right**. This becomes Springwater Road.
8.8 Turn **left** onto **Baker's Ferry Road**.
12.0 Cross Clackamas River.
12.5 Turn **right** to Barton Park.
13.5 Park road ends on the Clackamas River. Play in the park, then turn around and recross the bridge.
15.2 Turn **left** on **Eaden Road**.
19.4 T-intersection at **Springwater Road**, turn **left**.
22.0 Viewpoint to the left, restaurant and grocery to the right. Walk over to the fence at the viewpoint to see Mt. Hood, a bend in the Clackamas River, and McIver Park, your next destination.
23.9 Entrance to McIver Park. Because the descent to the river is 340 feet in 2.4 miles, going into the park is not included in the log.
24.2 Turn **right** on **Jubb Road.**
25.3 T-intersection at **Redland Road**, turn **left**.
26.2 The town of Viola. Turn **right** on **Mattoon Road**, just before Clear Creek. Or, for good views, a challenging climb and a swell descent keep

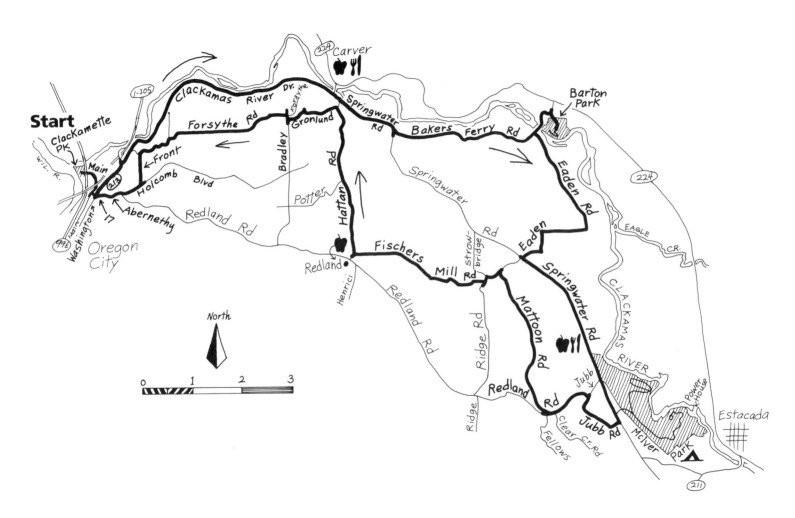

straight on Redland Road to the summit and take a sharp right on Ridge Road, adding .5 miles to your distance.

29.6 T-intersection at **Fischers Mill Road**, turn **left**.

30.0 Cross Clear Creek and turn **right**, staying on Fischers Mill Road (this is where Ridge Road comes in).

32.8 Turn **right** on **Hattan Road**.

35.9 Turn **left** on **Gronlund Road** at the chapel, after taking time to check out Bakers Log Cabin, built in 1856. Gronlund is a relentless 1.2 miles.

37.1 T-intersection at **Bradley Road**, turn **right**.

37.2 Intersection with **Forsythe Road**, turn **left**.

40.7 Stop sign at **Front Avenue**, turn **left**.

41.3 T-intersection at **Holcomb Boulevard**, turn **right**.

41.7 Stop sign, continue **straight** on **Abernethy Road**.

42.2 Cross Washington Street, staying on **17th Street**.

42.3 T-intersection at **Main Street**, turn **right**.

43.1 Return to **Clackamette Park**.

32 Sandy River

33 miles
from Troutdale
most difficult

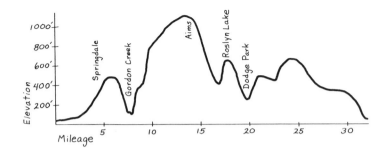

If you've ever hiked the Timberline Trail around Mt. Hood, you have seen the rugged power displayed at the headwaters of the Sandy River. On this bike ride along the lower Sandy, you see how the river with its power has carved a huge beautiful—and rugged— gorge. You will also see if your power can meet the river's challenge of the hills which are too steep, too long, and too many.

The views are, of course, as awesome and exhilarating as the climbs, and you go through some incredibly beautiful countryside. Dabney Park and Dodge Park along the route show parts of the river, but they don't convey the power of the river that this ride demonstrates.

0.0 Start at **Troutdale City Park** on Columbia Boulevard at the Sandy River. Head east and cross the river.

0.2 Turn **right** after the bridge staying on Crown Point Scenic Highway.

3.0 Dabney Park is to the right, situated on the Sandy River.

4.1 Town of Springdale.

4.3 Veer **right** to stay on the **Scenic Highway**.

4.5 Veer **right** onto **Hurlburt Road**.

6.5 Turn **right** with the main road on **Gordon Creek Road**.

13.9 Aims Museum of Relick's (sic) on the right. This museum contains artifacts from the neolithic and paleolithic eras.

14.5 Turn **right** on **Warriner Road** toward Dodge Park. This becomes Bull Run Road.

15.0 Road turns **left**.

17.0 Cross Bull Run River.

17.6 T-intersection at **Ten Eyck Road**, turn **right**. Roslyn Lake is to the left.

18.5 T-intersection at **Lusted Road**, turn **right**.

20.2 Dodge Park is on the right. Cross the Sandy River.

24.7 Turn **right** on **Hosner Road**.

25.2 Turn **left** onto **Oxbow Parkway**. If you instead continue straight, in two miles you get to Oxbow Park, another beautiful park on the Sandy River. It's a steep climb back up so we though we'd save Oxbow Park and campground for another trip.

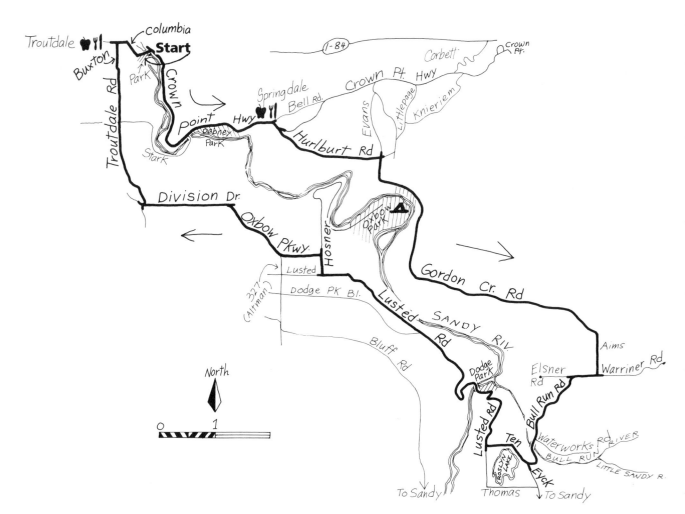

Troutdale
Columbia
Start
Buxton
Park
Crown
Troutdale Rd.
Stark
Point
Dabney
Park
Hwy
Springdale
Bell Rd.
Crown Pt. Hwy
Corbett
Crown Pt.
I-84
Evans
Littlepage
Knieriem
Hurlburt Rd
Division Dr.
Oxbow Pkwy.
Hosner
Oxbow Park
Lusted
327 (Altman)
Dodge Pk Bl.
Lusted Rd
Gordon Cr. Rd
SANDY RIV
Bluff Rd.
Aims
Warriner Rd.
Dodge Park
Elsner Rd.
North
0   1
Lusted Rd.
Ten
Eyck
Bull Run Rd
Waterworks Rd
BULL RUN RIVER
LITTLE SANDY R.
To Sandy
Roslyn Lake
Thomas
To Sandy

27.4 Oxbow Parkway becomes **Division Drive**.
28.9 Stop sign at **Troutdale Road**, turn **right**.
31.5 Troutdale Road becomes **Buxton Street**.
32.0 T-intersection at **Columbia Boulevard**, turn **right**.
32.6 Return to **Troutdale City Park**.

Dogs

Dogs and cyclists too often meet in unfavorable circumstances. Either the dog bites the pedaling leg, or the cyclist crashes into the yapping dog. Many avoidance tactics have been tried, with a variety of successes. Some cyclists sprint to out-run the dog, while some stop and dismount with the bicycle between them and the dog. Some bark back at the dog, some steer at the dog to overpower it. Many have tried the pump-waving technique to ward off the dog. Sometimes a directed squirt from the water bottle can deter a dog. A threatening dog on a regular commuting route can be quickly re-educated by squirting ammonia out of your water bottle, but don't be mistaken and drink from it.

33 Washougal River

**65 miles
from northeast Portland
most difficult
or
27 or 32 miles
from Camas, Washington
moderate**

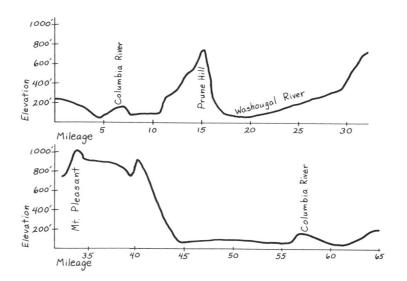

Mileage

Even for those of us who have ridden thousands of bike miles around the Portland area, it's still exciting to take a day ride and go to a new area that seems so distant and becalmed compared to Portland's pace. The road along the Washougal River is a beautiful, fairly level stretch, and then climbing the hills just south of the river is challenging and greatly rewarding. Along this latter section of farmlands you see easily twice as many horses as cars, and the views of the valleys and distant hills are relaxing.

This ride could be abbreviated for a shorter or flatter route in a couple ways. You could start in Camas, Washington (mile 17.0 in the log), making it a 32-mile loop. Or you could eliminate the steepest hills by turning around at the store (mile 29.7) and retracing the route rolling downstream with the

0.0 Portland's **Wilshire Park** is where to start, on N.E. 37th and Skidmore Street. Ride north on 37th for one block.
0.1 Stop sign at **Prescott Street**, turn **right**.
3.1 Turn **right** on the **bike path**, just after crossing the I-205 freeway.
3.1 Turn a sharp **right**, following the signs to Columbia Boulevard. Continue on the bike path following the signs through the Columbia Boulevard intersection.
4.7 Turn **left** toward Washington points.
7.5 Turn **right** onto **23rd Street** at the end of the bike path.
7.7 T-intersection at **Ellsworth Road**, turn **left** (following the sign "Bike Route SR-14 E.B." which means State Road #14 east bound).
7.8 Stop sign at **Evergreen Highway**, turn **left**.
10.9 Turn **left** as Evergreen Highway curves right, and turn **left** at the stop sign toward State Highway 14 (164th Avenue).

river. A longer option is to add the 15-mile round trip to Dougan Falls, which has a campground; follow the road from the store (mile 29.7) toward the Hatcheries and Dougan Falls.

Whatever loop you take along the Washougal River, you're sure to have a great bike ride.

11.4 Turn **right** on **34th Street**. This road is called 34th, Payne, 40th, Knight, 41st, 212th, 42nd, 224th, and 40th as you ride eastbound. It's all the same road without intersections, just different names.

15.2 Stop sign at **232nd Avenue**, turn **left**.

15.3 Turn **right** on **Forest Home Road**. This has a steep downhill run with a stop sign at the end where you can barely stop.

16.2 Turn **left** on **10th Avenue**.

16.5 T-intersection at **Drake Street**, turn **right**.

16.7 Stop sign at **7th Avenue**, turn **left**, then **right** to Drake.

16.7 Stop sign at **6th Avenue**, turn **left**.

17.0 Stop sign at **Adams Street**, turn **right**.

17.2 Turn **left** on **3rd Avenue**.

18.8 Turn **left** on **Sheperd Road**.

20.0 T-intersection at **Washougal River Road** (Highway 140), turn **left**.

29.7 Turn **right** with Highway 140 by the store, and cross the river. Or you can stay left following the signs to Hatcheries and Dougan Falls for an extra 15-mile loop.

30.5 Prindle County Park, a nice picnic spot by a creek.

32.7 Turn **right** on **Mt. Pleasant Road**.

34.8 Turn **right** as the road curves at **Belle Center Road**. This is called Gibson Road in Clark County.

37.3 After the county line, turn **right** on **Turner Road**, during a quick downhill. This becomes 410th, 30th, Moffet Road.

39.4 T-intersection at **35th Street**, turn **right**.

39.7 35th turns **right** and becomes **377th Avenue**.

39.8 Turn **right** as Sunset View curves left, and stay on **377th Avenue**.

40.5 T-intersection at **20th Street**, turn **left**.

41.9 Four-way intersection at **352nd Avenue**, turn **left**. This is another road that is continous despite its various names: 352nd, Jennings, 347th, Lawton, 34th, Stiles, and 32nd. But you can ride down fast without worrying about the names.

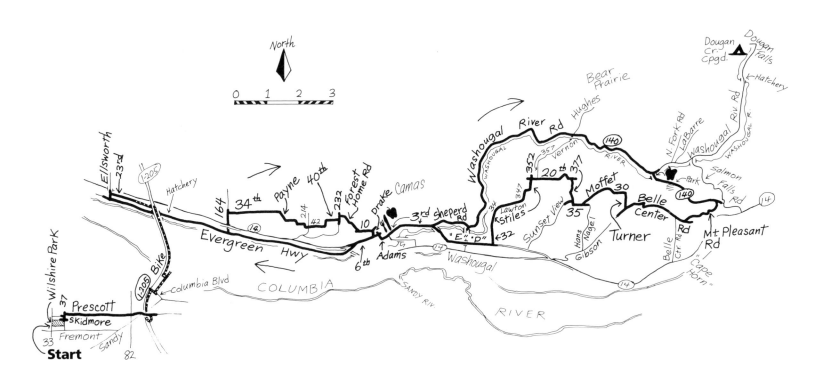

44.9 Stop sign on **D Street**, turn **right**. D Street becomes E Street, and then 3rd Avenue.

48.6 Turn **right** on **Adams Street**.

48.8 Turn **left** on **6th Avenue**.

49.8 Turn **left** on **6th/Evergreen Highway**. The sign says "Washougal S.R. Eastbound."

53.9 Stay **left** at the fork (164th Avenue) to stay on Evergreen Highway.

56.9 Turn **right** on **Ellsworth Road**.

57.0 Turn **right** on **23rd Street**.

57.3 Turn **left** onto the bike path at the sign, and cross the Columbia River.

60.1 Turn **right** toward Columbia Boulevard.

61.6 Turn **left** from the bike path toward Prescott Street.

61.7 Turn **left** on **Prescott Street**.

64.7 Turn **left** at **37th Avenue**.

64.8 Return to **Wilshire Park**, 37th and Skidmore Street.

34 Silver Creek Falls

Campground for overnight
50 miles each day
from Oregon City
most difficult

Going camping at Silver Falls State Park is a real vacation. Not that it isn't work to get there; but the route passes through various delightful farms, small towns and a forest, while the park itself is a vast expanse of views, trails, waterfalls, wildlife, and even a swimming hole.

Silver Falls is a popular camping spot, and reservations are on a first come, first served basis. The campground is open May through October, and indeed there may be snow the remaining months.

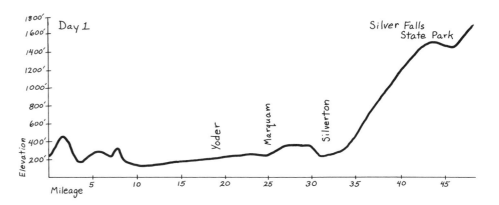

Day 1

0.0 Begin at the **library** in Oregon City, 6th and Adams Street. Ride south on Adams one block.

0.1 Stop sign at **5th Street**, turn **left**. This becomes **Linn Avenue**.

1.5 Turn **right** on **Central Point Road**.

7.7 Turn **right** on **Township Road**.

10.8 T-intersection at **Ivy Street**, turn **left**. This becomes Canby-Marquam Road, and later Kropf Road.

19.6 Town of Yoder.

24.6 Stop sign at **Highway 213** (Marquam), turn **right** toward Silverton. This is called Oak Street in Silverton.

31.6 T-intersection at **Highway 214** in Silverton, turn **left** toward Silver Falls State Park.

45.6 North Falls Trailhead.

46.1 North Falls viewpoint. Soon you encounter the bike path which meanders toward the park lodge.

47.9 Park lodge is to the right. Continue straight.

48.2 Turn **left** into the **campground**.

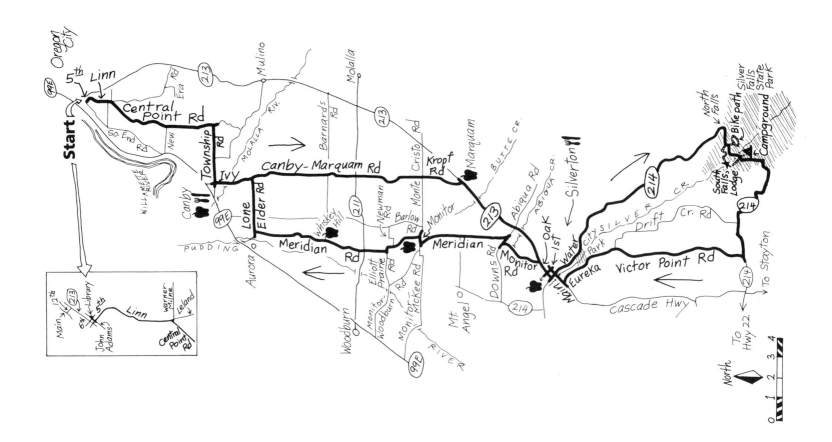

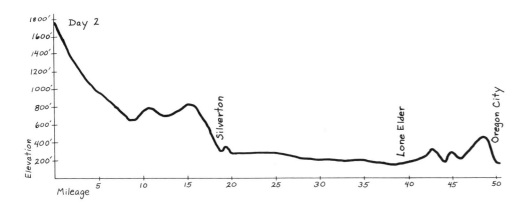

Day 2

- **0.0** Leave the campground turning **left** on **Highway 214**.
- **7.6** Turn **right** on **Victor Point Road**, as Highway 214 curves left.
- **14.9** Stop sign where Drift Creek Road comes in, curve **left** and stay on **Victor Point Road**. This is called Eureka Avenue in Silverton.
- **18.3** T-intersection at **Main Street**, turn **right** to Silverton city center.
- **18.4** Stop sign at **First Street**, turn **left** toward Highway 213.
- **18.4** Four-way stop sign at **Oak Street**, turn **right**.
- **19.3** Turn **left** on **Monitor Road**. This becomes Meridian Road.
- **20.0** Stop sign where Hobart Road comes in, continue **straight** on **Meridian Road**.
- **26.3** Stop sign at **Woodburn-Monitor Road**, turn **right**. Town of Monitor.
- **26.4** Turn **left** on **Meridian Road**.
- **28.7** Turn **right**, rather than go straight, to stay on **Meridian Road**.
- **36.3** T-intersection at **Lone Elder Road**, turn **right**.
- **39.2** T-intersection at **Canby-Marquam Highway**, turn **left** toward Oregon City. This becomes Ivy Street in Canby.
- **39.4** Turn **right** on **Township Road**.

42.5 T-intersection at **Central Point Road**, turn **left**.

48.7 Stop sign at **Linn Avenue**, turn **left**. This becomes 5th Street.

50.1 Turn **right** on **Adams Street**.

50.2 Return to the **library**, 6th and Adams Street.

Index